Celebrate Louisiana's Seasonal Bounty

Few places are more closely tied to the rhythms of the seasons than Louisiana's River Parishes, which stretch along the levees of the Mississippi River between New Orleans and Baton Rouge. From hunting and fishing to harvesting the plentiful crops that thrive under the South's warm sun, the abundance provided by Louisiana's lands and waterways is crafted into delectable dishes by the families who have cultivated this area of the state for generations.

Chef Jarred Zeringue, proprietor of Wayne Jacob's Smokehouse, celebrates that bounty in this approachable guide to Cajun cooking. Featuring the flavors and culture he learned from his large extended family, Jarred offers an intimate window into how they—like so many in Louisiana's River Parishes—cook from the land, using the freshest ingredients in a lifestyle that embodies the farm to table philosophy.

With nearly 90 recipes divided by the seasons, Jarred shares the traditional tastes of his childhood, with an emphasis on the smoked meats for which his smokehouse is renowned.

SOUTHERN AND SMOKED

SOUTHERN AND SMOKED

CAJUN COOKING THROUGH THE SEASONS

JARRED I. ZERINGUE

PELICAN PUBLISHING
New Orleans 2022

Photography by Denny Culbert and Joseph Vidrine.
Historical images on pages 8-9, 25, 44-45, 140, and 197 are by the author's ancestor, Olide P. Schexnayder.

The word "Pelican" and the depiction of a pelican are trademarks of Arcadia Publishing Company Inc. and are registered in the U.S. Patent and Trademark Office.

ISBN: 9781455626380
Ebook ISBN: 9781455626397

Printed in Korea

Published by Pelican Publishing
New Orleans, LA
www.pelicanpub.com

Thank you to all who helped with this book and to all who came before me, paving the way for me to do what I love.

To my parents, who love unconditionally and support me even when I seem to bite off more than I can chew. Their worries, their prayers, and their concern keep me moving forward so that I can make them proud.

CONTENTS

A NOTE TO MY READERS

My family has lived, worked, and farmed in the River Parishes of Louisiana and nearby New Orleans from as early as 1720. That year the Zeringue family immigrated from Alsace. The following year, the Schexnayder family from Belgium began to call Louisiana home and Chauvin family members began to make their way from France through Nova Scotia. Fifty years later, in 1771 the Tassins followed the Chauvins from France. In the River Parishes, the blend of Cajun, Creole, German, French, Spanish, African, and Native American cultures have influenced the dishes we make. We have been blessed with a rich culture of cooking, eating, farming, hunting, and fishing.

Today I honor that tradition in my restaurants and at Wayne Jacob's Smokehouse. Located in LaPlace, Louisiana, the "Andouille Capital of the World," the smokehouse has been passed down through generations of locals who, with great attention to tradition and quality, continue its history of continually producing the highest quality artisan-smoked meats and fresh sausage. Even after the devastation wrought by Hurricane Ida in 2021, we continue to serve the community

the traditional meats that feature so prominently in the Cajun and Creole dishes of Louisiana's River Parishes.

As you flip through the pages of this book, I hope to connect you with my community's and my family's way of life and to illustrate how our menus, so connected to all that the land has to offer, change with the seasons. Together we'll explore each season through recipes containing items that are fresh, in season, and therefore cost effective. I'll also show you how to utilize and preserve some seasonal items through canning or freezing. I hope the recipes and photographs inspire you to go into the garden or market and grow, use, or buy local and seasonal items.

These recipes are intended for the casual cook, those who learned the basics by their grandmother's side or gleaned grilling tips from family get-togethers, but I also hope this book will be a great resource to anyone interested in learning about traditional Cajun cooking. However, instead of presenting another Louisiana cooking encyclopedia, I want to instead offer an intimate window into how a family—my family—celebrates the seasons.

The family homestead.
Courtesy of the Collections of the Louisiana State Museum, 1998.001.16.007

INTRODUCTION

In South Louisiana, almost 300 years ago, our ancestors fought to make this place a home. Some came as speculators in search of riches, some came as prisoners banished from their home country, some were brought as enslaved workers, and some were native to these shores. They left an indelible mark on the people, culture, and food traditions of those who call this area home today. Even now, we employ many of the traditional techniques, ingredients, and customs of each of these cultures. In my family, as in most, there are slight differences in how my grandmothers prepare the same dishes, their recipes influenced by their differing heritage. Where I'm from there are amazing cooks, with both women and men taking great pride in what they literally bring to the table.

Between hunting, fishing, farming, and gardening there always seems to be bounty from Mother Nature. Our subtropical climate ensures that no matter the season, there will always be something fresh to eat. This book is a journey through a year of seasonal farming, cooking, and celebrating in the River Parishes and South Louisiana. It is an effort to preserve some of the

recipes, food traditions, and culture that we hold dear. In an increasingly high-speed world filled with an expectation of instant gratification, bumper sticker mantras, and social media moments, we need to be reminded that almost everything we do is part of the continuum of our forebearers' hard work and history. In writing this book I hope to recognize the tireless efforts of the people who came before me, who through many adversities kept moving forward to provide, nurture, and build upon the traditions we celebrate today.

The name of my hometown in Cajun French is *la Vacherie* and refers to the cow pasture, as this area was high ground on the west bank of the Mississippi River used for cattle farming. The town of Vacherie, originally named Tabiscanja ("long river view") by the Colapissa Indians, has also been known as St. Patrick and St. Philip over the years. Vacherie was a mélange of cultures where the downriver Germans and the upriver Acadians blended to create a French-speaking community in the heart of Creole Louisiana. As its early plantation economy developed, enslaved peoples from West Africa and

the Caribbean contributed many of the lasting influences on the food traditions of the region. Sugar, indigo, cotton, soybeans, rice, tobacco, and many fruits and vegetables have been grown in the region's fertile soil, and some of these crops are still farmed here. Bound on the south by rich swamps of Lac des Allemands, here seafood and many forms of wild game are also plentiful. Nestled among the cane fields of St. James Parish, today the small community of Vacherie is home to historic plantation sites and large extended families that thrive on the opportunity to share their cuisine of old recipes with those who visit.

Both my mother and father grew up in St. John the Baptist Parish, Louisiana. Although raised only seven miles apart, from early ages they had different views of how the world worked. My mother's relatives lived in Edgard. They were a large family with a small sugarcane farm. Her grandfather Philip Eloi Chauvin was the immediate family's sole survivor of the yellow fever epidemic that struck South Louisiana. He was from a town that still bears his surname. After the rest of his family died, when he was around the age of 15, he moved to Edgard to live with relatives.

Philip's great-grandfather, Xiste Jean Baptiste Dumez, had lived in Edgard since he was exiled to Louisiana from France for writing against the government. He learned nothing from this punishment as not long after he settled, he started a newspaper called *La Mechachebe* (translated as "*The Shit-Stirrer*"), which operated into the 1950s.

My great-grandfather married Esperance Leroux from Reserve and they had 12 children. He bought his farm for $6,900 in 1945 and paid it off in less than eight years thanks to his wife's meticulous bookkeeping. Many of their children bought parcels of the family farm, where they raised their own families.

My grandfather Philip Chauvin, Jr. married my grandmother Winnie Rose Tassin, also from Edgard. My grandfather served in the Korean War, where he worked as a chauffeur for some of the top brass. Family stories tell of him once driving off the side of a mountain and frequently wrecking automobiles. The man I knew as my grandfather was more of a daredevil than careless, and it is that trait to which I attribute his questionable driving record.

He returned from Korea but contracted encephalitis in 1953. He was in and out of comas and suffered lasting effects from his illness. He lived in the New Orleans Home for the Incurables until 1975, when my grandmother brought him back home and cared for him with the help of a sitter. For the duration of his stay in New Orleans, my grandmother hauled four children on a bus from Edgard every Sunday to see him.

As a result of her husband's disability, Winnie was essentially a single mother in the 1950s and '60s. She put herself through secretarial school and supported their family on her own. She worked as the secretary at Edgard School and West St. John High School until the late 1990s. She cooked large batches of food so that she could put food in the freezer for my grandfather and his sitter to eat

while she worked. Her freezer was a card catalogue of everything she had cooked in the previous months. She always had an amazing selection of her delicious foods in single-serving packs. She was an amazing cook, as was her brother Lewis Tassin. His gumbo, jambalaya, and bread pudding recipes are the bases for mine today. He learned woodworking from their father Isaie Tassin, who was also the town barber. I have his barber chair and share his name, Isaie, as my middle name.

As my grandfather's motor skills improved he became an escape artist. After he stole his brother's truck to drive to the store to buy cigarettes, taking out every mailbox along the way, my grandma put up an eight-foot fence around the yard. He soon scaled it. Barbed wire was added, and he still found a way to get out. It wasn't until he was too old to bother that he settled for waving to passing cars while my grandmother was at work. A few times, he flagged down passing ambulances. When the driver asked, "Mr. Chauvin, is everything okay?" (it is that small of a town), he was laughing so hard he could hardly catch his breath. But when he did, he asked them for a cigarette.

My father's family lived in Wallace, seven miles upriver from Edgard. He grew up in a multi-generational household on our family's sugarcane farm, where he worked from a young age. Even though they were German and French by blood, Cajun French was predominately spoken in the house as this was the language of business and gossip in the area. My grandfather Rene Zeringue was a cook during World War II and served in Okinawa. Upon his return, he and two friends bought a parcel of land to farm. It was about 50 acres and forested. The three cleared the land and farmed sugarcane. At times they also harvested soybeans, rice, crawfish, and potatoes. He married my grandmother Noelie Schexnayder and moved into her multi-generational family's house. They raised their children with the help and influence of her mother, Winceslas Simon Schexnayder, her sister Anabell, and cousins that all lived under the same roof.

My grandfather understood the concept of service to others and was deeply involved in the community. He was even elected as head of the police jury. When my grandmother, Noelie, unexpectedly passed away at the age of thirty-six, he would eventually marry her sister Anabell, the only grandmother I knew on that side. Although German influence led to a much stricter household than the more relaxed French Creole influence of my mother's family, and neither love nor death was talked about openly in that household, Anabell would do anything for us and, without question, cared for us as her own.

This rich family background, with its French and German ancestry, stoked my love for the food and folkways of South Louisiana. This love bleeds into the food I cook for my family, for my friends, and for the members of the community who gather around the table at my restaurants and at Wayne Jacob's Smokehouse. I invite you to try the meals my community has enjoyed for generations and experience the taste, flavors, and charm of Louisiana's Cajun Country.

RULES OF THE CAJUN KITCHEN

Here are a few rules I've gathered from my family's kitchens or have learned the hard way.

1. First You Make a Roux.

Use oil or bacon fat for roux that is the basis for a dish with red meat, pork, or poultry. A butter roux should be used with seafood or vegetables. The stronger the meat, the darker the roux. A good Cajun cook would never overpower a dish of valuable ingredients with a roux.

Roux can be made in larger quantities and stored in the freezer for future use.

2. Worship the Trinity.

The traditional Cajun trinity is 2 parts onion, 1 part celery, and 1 part bell pepper. In my seasoning, I almost always include or even substitute 1 part shallot tops or green onions, 1 part flat leaf parsley, and a bit of garlic. Consider the proteins in the dish and be careful not to overpower them with seasonings.

Save time during the week by chopping aromatics in bulk and storing them in the freezer. As long as the proportions are correct, you can mix all the seasonings together in a large bowl and portion them into quart or gallon size bags. Lay flat and stack to freeze.

3. Build the Flavor.

Cajun cooking is all about building flavors from simple ingredients. Food without color is food without flavor. Just as it is important to cook with the correct seasonings, it is equally important to treat the seasonings correctly to achieve the optimum caramelization and flavor. The browning of ingredients will stop immediately when liquid is added, and the flavor will dissolve into the liquid. Understanding each ingredient, how it plays into the dish, and how to coerce the best flavors out of it are signs of a good cook.

Chicken skin and bones, beef bones and fat, vegetable scraps, and parsley stems are all great ingredients to make stocks. Stocks are the perfect way to not only cook with less waste, they are also the secret to preparing full-flavored dishes.

4. A Watched Pot . . .

Cajun cooking requires patience. It is imperative to taste, smell, and monitor the color, flavor, and consistency of a dish throughout the cooking process. Standing over the pot is not necessary, but checking on the level of heat and checking for overheating and sticking is. Seasoning along the way is also key. Keeping everything on track and being patient is much easier than trying to rescue a dish that has been ruined.

5. Eat in Season.

Food traditions are based on seasonal availability. When we eat things that are in season, we get the freshest ingredients and the best taste, all at the best price.

6. Share the Love.

As with all cultures, South Louisiana cooking is a celebration of life, family, and tradition. We cook to share the rewards of hard work, to bring people together, to honor those who have come before us, and to pass the traditions on to future generations.

Cook enough to give away to neighbors, friends, and family. It costs little more time, effort, or money to share with others, and the impact may be more than you may realize.

7. Spice It Up.

After years of both training cooks in my restaurants and writing recipes, I decided to make a go-to spice mix for consistency and predictability. It is very simple and will cut a few steps out of your cooking process. It consists of 6 ingredients.

Circle Z Seasoning Mix
1 part kosher salt
1 part black pepper
1 part onion powder
1 part garlic powder
¼ part cayenne pepper
¼ part ground bay leaf

Mix all ingredients together and store in an airtight container.

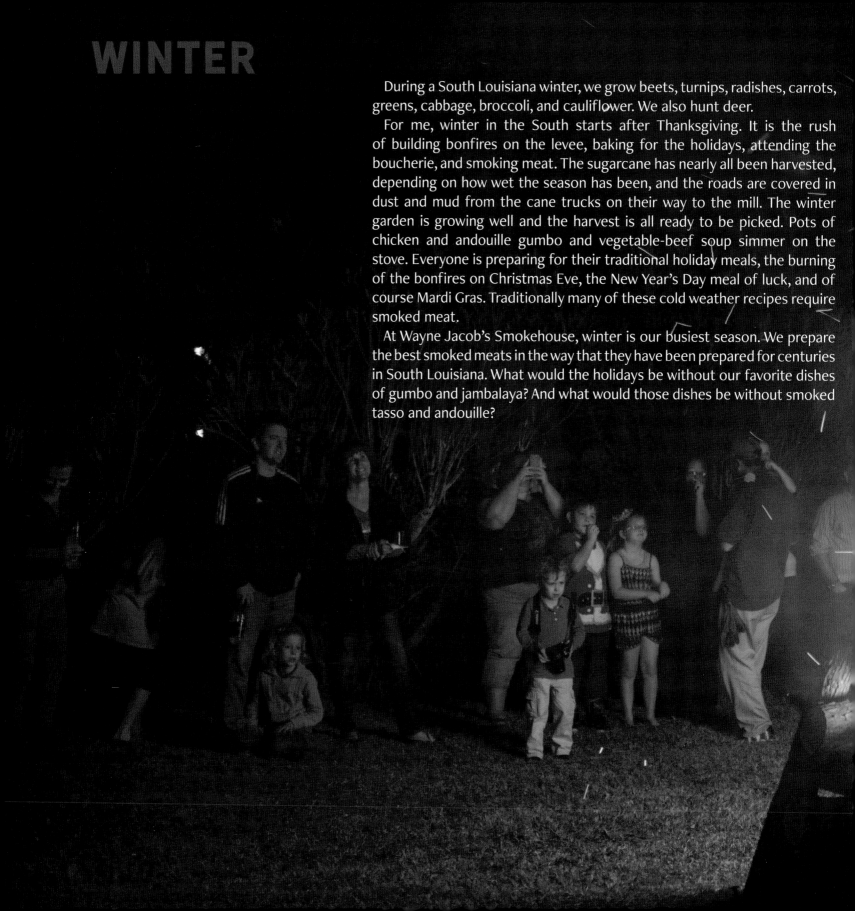

WINTER

During a South Louisiana winter, we grow beets, turnips, radishes, carrots, greens, cabbage, broccoli, and cauliflower. We also hunt deer.

For me, winter in the South starts after Thanksgiving. It is the rush of building bonfires on the levee, baking for the holidays, attending the boucherie, and smoking meat. The sugarcane has nearly all been harvested, depending on how wet the season has been, and the roads are covered in dust and mud from the cane trucks on their way to the mill. The winter garden is growing well and the harvest is all ready to be picked. Pots of chicken and andouille gumbo and vegetable-beef soup simmer on the stove. Everyone is preparing for their traditional holiday meals, the burning of the bonfires on Christmas Eve, the New Year's Day meal of luck, and of course Mardi Gras. Traditionally many of these cold weather recipes require smoked meat.

At Wayne Jacob's Smokehouse, winter is our busiest season. We prepare the best smoked meats in the way that they have been prepared for centuries in South Louisiana. What would the holidays be without our favorite dishes of gumbo and jambalaya? And what would those dishes be without smoked tasso and andouille?

TIP:

YOU CAN PICKLE NEARLY ANY VEGETABLE. SOME OF MY FAVORITES INCLUDE GREEN BEANS, CUCUMBERS, CAULIFLOWER, OKRA, BRUSSELS SPROUTS, RED ONIONS, RADISHES, TURNIPS, GREEN TOMATOES, AND CARROTS.

Pickled vegetables are my favorite snack. Since almost anything can be pickled, this is one solution to dealing with the bounty of summer and winter gardens. Use them on sandwiches, battered and fried, accompanying white beans and fresh sausage, or in a Bloody Mary.

6 quarts of vegetables,
   cut into bite-size pieces
2 cups white vinegar
½ cup salt
3 tbsp. sugar (optional)
1 tbsp. dill seed
3 tbsp. whole black peppercorns

1 tbsp. red pepper flakes
12 whole garlic cloves
2 tbsp. mustard seeds
2 tbsp. coriander seeds
¼ cup sriracha sauce
   (optional for spice)

Combine all ingredients in a large non-reactive pot (ceramic, glass, or stainless steel) with 1 gallon of water. Boil for 30 minutes. Ladle hot liquid, including seeds and garlic, over fresh vegetables. Either jar the vegetables or let cool in an airtight container then refrigerate.

Makes 6 quarts.

CHEDDAR PECAN CRACKERS

Each year on the Sunday before Christmas, thousands of people gather in Jackson Square to sing Christmas carols. When I opened Vacherie Restaurant in the French Quarter, I decided to hold a Christmas open house for family, friends, employees, and neighbors to enjoy holiday treats and eggnog before heading out to sing. Over the years the menu has grown along with the size of the crowd. Some of the original snacks on that menu were Cheddar Pecan Crackers, Hog Head Cheese, and Smoked Chicken Liver Pâté.

1 cup butter, melted
1 cup pecan pieces
¼ cup black sesame seeds
16 oz. sharp Cheddar cheese, grated
1 tsp. cayenne
1½ tbsp. Circle Z Seasoning Mix (see Index)
20 dashes Tabasco
2 cups flour
1 tsp. baking powder

Preheat oven to 350 degrees. In a large bowl combine all ingredients to create a dough. Shape dough by ½ tablespoonfuls into balls and arrange on a baking sheet lined with aluminum foil. Flatten slightly and bake for 20-25 minutes until slightly golden on the edges. Cool before removing from foil.

Makes about 40 crackers.

HOG HEAD CHEESE

Every year in January or February, my family holds a boucherie. Hog head cheese is one of the first items started during the festivities because it cooks for hours and then has to set for several more. Cajun pâté is how I explain this dish to "foreigners." There aren't many things in life better than a few slices of hog head cheese, a few saltine crackers, spicy pickled vegetables, and a cold beer. This recipe has been adapted to a home kitchen because the original recipe calls for gelatin from the butchered pig's skin and bones, which may not be readily available from your local market.

1 pork butt	1 tsp. onion powder
1 onion, diced	1 tsp. garlic powder
1 cup diced peppers	1 tsp. ground bay leaf
6 garlic cloves, smashed	1 tsp. paprika
1 tsp. red pepper flakes	5 green onions, finely chopped
1 tsp. cayenne pepper	1 red pepper, finely chopped
2 tsp. black pepper	½ cup unflavored gelatin dissolved in 4 cups
4 tsp. salt	cold water

Fill a large stockpot with 1 gallon of water. Add first 12 ingredients and bring to a simmer. Simmer for at least 2 hours, or until pork falls apart. Remove meat from stock and transfer to a mixing bowl. Roughly chop the meat then mix in green onions and red pepper. Set aside. Strain stock, discarding the vegetables, and return stock to pot. Stir gelatin mixture into the hot stock. Add pork mixture to stock and simmer for 10 minutes. Pour into molds or loaf pans, cover, and refrigerate overnight until firm.

Yields about 8 lb.

SMOKED CHICKEN LIVER PÂTÉ

People either love liver or they don't. I don't, so I tried smoking it. As much as I love smoked meats, I figured the smoking process could only improve the flavor. In fact, it added a great, unexpected aspect to this pâté, which has become a popular holiday item at the smokehouse. Even if you don't have access to smoked chicken livers, it is still a great recipe.

1 large onion, thinly sliced
¼ tsp. allspice
2 tsp. salt
2 tsp. black pepper
½ cup butter, divided
1 lb. smoked chicken livers

½ cup chicken broth
3 eggs, boiled and peeled
1 bunch parsley, chopped
1 tbsp. cognac
6 tbsp. heavy cream

In a large pan over medium heat, sauté onion, allspice, salt, and pepper in 1 tbsp. butter. Add smoked chicken livers and chicken broth. Bring to a boil and then reduce heat to low. Simmer for 10 minutes then remove from heat and allow to cool.

In a food processor, chop eggs and parsley until very fine. Add the cooled chicken and onion mixture. Continue processing while slowly adding cognac, heavy cream, and remaining butter. Process until smooth. Turn out into a pan or mold lined with plastic wrap. Chill in the refrigerator until set, at least 3 hours.

Makes 6 cups.

Opposite: South Louisiana residents enjoy a picnic, late 1890s.
Courtesy of the Collections of the Louisiana State Museum, 1998.001.16.024

My family looked forward to the yearly boucherie, usually held in early February. As small kids we dressed the night before and slept in our clothes. My dad would get us out of bed wrapped in a blanket at about 4:00 A.M. and carry us to the truck, where we would sleep until awoken by the sound of a .22 gunshot and a pig's squeals. At that time, we'd put on our shoes—if my dad hadn't forgotten them—and head out to join the rest of the family. We didn't want to miss the action.

The pig was always killed just before the sun came up. No matter how many times this tradition was carried out, there was always disagreement about the best way to go about it. The definition for boucherie should be the act of killing a pig with too many chefs and not enough helpers. But we always had the same outcome: delicious food for everyone to take home and universal exhaustion.

Here's a brief rundown of the process: At about 3:00 A.M., Uncle Jimmy arrives to start boiling the giant pots of water, get coffee going, set up work tables, and sharpen knives. An hour later, the next wave of early people, his brothers and family, show up to unload their cooking pots and critique the way things have been set up. By 5:00 A.M. families arrive with sleeping kids in tow. They help unload and set up while sipping coffee and telling tales of boucheries past. Finally, around 5:30, everyone prepares to shoot the pig. This is always preceded by a discussion on how best to do so as well as a last-minute decision on whether or not the pig will be bled to make blood boudin.

Once the pig has been dispatched and hung by the hind legs, the pace of things starts to pick up. Curious kids start to emerge from the trucks to investigate the activity. Boiling water is poured over the pig, which is then shaved with a knife to remove its coarse hair. The pig is then cut from tail to neck and its organs carefully removed. If any part of the digestive system is punctured, it

Carrying on a tradition: boucheries past and present.

could contaminate the meat. The head is removed and moved to a different station to begin making the hog head cheese. The belly is removed and cut into long strips. As kids we were given these strips and very large knives to cut for cracklins. When we finished that important job, we were invited into the house where Aunt Marie-Therese made keks with butter and cane syrup for our breakfast. While we were having breakfast, the cracklins were frying, the hog head cheese was simmering, the blood sausage was getting stuffed, and the meat for the andouille and sausage was getting chopped and ground. Despite any disagreements, each station in the boucherie was always manned and usually people would gravitate toward the same station year after year.

The beer started to flow by about 10:00. By noon the Cajun band had struck up its first chords or someone's truck radio would be blasting zydeco and swamp pop. Some started to dance in the driveway as they finished their work. As 3:00 P.M. neared, everything but the smoking of the sausage was complete and it was time to rest and have a good time.

When my relatives showed up to my recent boucherie, they brought pictures from the 1950 boucherie held at my cousin's house. The photographs showed my grandparents, unmarried and on their way to a date in Donaldsonville. My great-aunts and great-grandmother were all photographed at their work. It was a pretty amazing surprise to see this history while we carried on the family tradition.

VEGETABLE-BEEF SOUP

At the first sign of a frost, my mom would make one of two things: Vegetable-Beef Soup or Chicken and Andouille Gumbo. I guess what she made depended on whether it was too early to harvest what she needed from the garden or if we were up to our ears in vegetables. Either way we knew the big Magnalite pot was coming out and it would be an all-day thing. However much we ate that day would not even make a dent in the pot's contents. There was always a lot to freeze and a lot to give away.

5 tbsp. Circle Z Seasoning Mix, divided (see Index)
4 tbsp. flour
2 lb. lean stew meat, cubed
4 strips Wayne Jacob's bacon, chopped
1 tbsp. celery salt
2 cups diced onions
1 cup sliced green onions
1 cup diced celery
1 cup diced bell pepper
1 tbsp. chopped garlic
1 lb. baby carrots, sliced

24 oz. canned diced tomatoes
4 oz. tomato paste
2 quarts beef stock
2 tbsp. Worcestershire sauce
1 tsp. thyme
1 head of green cabbage, cored and chopped
1 head of broccoli, chopped
½ lb. baby lima beans
½ lb. corn
½ lb. baby green beans
½ lb. pasta (I prefer a smaller pasta so it fits on the spoon)
½ lb. frozen peas

In a shallow bowl, combine 2 tbsp. seasoning mix with flour. Dredge stew meat in flour and set aside. In a large soup pot over medium heat, render bacon. When crispy, remove bacon from pot and set aside. Add stew meat to pot and brown in bacon fat. Add celery salt, onions, green onions, celery, bell pepper, garlic, and carrots to pot and sweat until onions are translucent. Mix in diced tomatoes, tomato paste, beef stock, Worcestershire sauce, remaining seasoning mix, and thyme. Carefully add 1 gallon of water. Bring to a boil and add the remaining vegetables. Reduce temperature to low and simmer until beef is tender . Add pasta, peas, and crispy bacon once beef is fork tender. Add more water as needed.

Makes 8 quarts

TIP:
YOU MAY SUBSTITUTE FROZEN—NOT CANNED—VEGETABLES FOR ANY THAT ARE NOT AVAILABLE FRESH.

WAYNE JACOB'S CHICKEN AND ANDOUILLE GUMBO

Chicken and andouille gumbo is why I do what I do. It is the cornerstone of traditional South Louisiana food. The very act of cooking it is the essence of tradition and community. No one makes a small gumbo, so every time I cook a large pot, I think about the people who will be eating it. I think about the holidays and celebrations enjoyed with gumbo. I think about the customers who are trying it for the first time as well as those who are transported back to their childhoods in their mother's or grandmother's kitchen as they taste it.

Gumbo season starts at the first cool front and lasts until Mardi Gras, with the peak at Christmas. It is the tradition on the Mississippi River to burn bonfires on the levee on Christmas Eve. In most River Parish kitchens, chicken and andouille gumbo simmers on the stove all day, to be enjoyed after the bonfires or even after Midnight Mass. No gumbo would be complete without Coco's filé. Coco, a Wayne Jacob's mainstay and nephew of the smokehouse's original owner, picks the sassafras leaves at just the right time then dries and grinds them to the most vibrant green. I am sure the filé sold commercially contains the same ingredients, but over time the color fades as well as the flavor. With filé, fresh is much better.

This recipe is for a traditional Cajun Country gumbo. It differs from New Orleans-style gumbo in that it is thinner and more brothy. You can make it to your liking by adding more or less stock or roux.

1 cup flour	1 lb. Wayne Jacob's smoked sausage, sliced
1 cup canola oil	1 lb. Wayne Jacob's andouille, sliced
1½ large yellow onions, diced	2 lb. Wayne Jacob's smoked chicken, cubed
4 stalks celery, diced	3 tbsp. Worcestershire sauce
2 green bell peppers, diced	3 tbsp. Circle Z Seasoning Mix (see Index)
1 bunch green onions, chopped	2 tsp. gumbo filé
1 bunch Italian parsley, chopped	2 bay leaves
1 clove garlic, minced	3 quarts chicken stock

In an 8 quart pot combine flour and canola oil. Cook over medium heat, constantly stirring and scraping the bottom of the pot until the roux is the color of caramel. Add vegetables and cook until onions are translucent. Stir in sausage, andouille, chicken, Worcestershire, seasoning mixture, and filé and cook until meat starts to caramelize. Add chicken stock and cook, partially covered, over low heat for 3 hours, stirring occasionally.

Makes 6 quarts.

POTATO SALAD

In the River Parishes, we eat our potato salad in our gumbo. This is a very simple recipe, but you can fancy it up by adding whatever extras you like. I don't really care for crunchy things in my potato salad, but many people add celery, green onions, or fresh parsley.

2 lb. red potatoes, cubed
6 eggs, boiled and peeled
3 tbsp. dill relish
3 tbsp. chopped jalapeño peppers
1 tbsp. Circle Z Seasoning Mix (see Index)
1 cup mayonnaise
¼ cup Creole mustard

In a large pot, boil potatoes until fork tender; drain and remove to a large mixing bowl. Mix together remaining ingredients and fold into hot boiled potatoes. Serve as a side or in gumbo.

Makes 3 quarts.

WHITE BEANS

This is one of the simplest recipes in the book and takes about five minutes of prep work. I tend to make this dish vegetarian although salt pork, bacon, or sausage are delicious additions.

My Mama Bell cooked two pounds of white beans per week throughout her entire adult life. I guess that her German heritage, and the need to feed a family of farmers, led her to prepare hearty meals. She would soak her beans overnight in a bowl on the counter and start cooking them at about 5:00 A.M. Lunch was always ready at 11:00 A.M. sharp. While lunch was cooking, she would do all of her washing and cleaning. I loved waking up to the smell of cooking beans and a roast browning.

1 onion, chopped
1 tbsp. salt
2 tsp. black pepper
1 tsp. cayenne pepper
1 lb. Navy beans or Great Northern
   beans, soaked overnight
3 tbsp. canola oil

In a 6 quart pot over medium heat, sauté onion and seasonings in canola oil until onions are translucent. Add beans and 3 quarts of water to the pot. Bring beans to a boil and then cover and reduce heat to low until beans are creamy, about 2 hours, stirring every 20 minutes to prevent sticking. Beans that are cooked covered on a lower fire will be creamier with less chance of sticking.

Makes 3 quarts.

NEW YEAR'S BLACK-EYED PEAS

My Papa Rene used to swear that eating black-eyed peas on New Year's Day was the only way to ward off the "red mange." I have no idea what red mange entails, but it sounds bad enough that I will be eating my peas.

Black-eyed peas have more of a muddy flavor than other beans so I cook them with a roux and Wayne Jacob's smoked sausage. Because this recipe is roux-based, it will have a thicker and more creamy consistency. On the side I always provide smothered cabbage for wealth and cornbread for luck. New Year's Day is the perfect day for such a healing meal; it wards off the hangover from New Year's Eve celebrations.

1 smoked ham hock (optional)
½ cup canola oil or bacon grease
½ cup flour
1 large onion, diced
1 bunch green onions, chopped
1 bunch Italian parsley, chopped
1 lb. Wayne Jacob's smoked sausage
   cut into rounds
3 tbsp. Circle Z Seasoning Mix (see Index)
2 tbsp. Worcestershire sauce
1 lb. dried black-eyed peas or
   2 lb. frozen or fresh peas

To make the stock combine 3 quarts water and smoked ham hock in a large pot; bring to a boil then reduce to a simmer. Allow stock to simmer while you prepare the peas.

In a Dutch oven over medium heat, combine oil and flour to make a roux. Cook, stirring constantly, until the roux turns a caramel color. Stir in onion, green onions, parsley, sausage, seasoning mix, and Worcestershire sauce. Cook until onions are translucent and sausage starts to brown, stirring often to prevent sticking. The longer you fry the sausage in the roux mixture, the more smoke flavor you will enjoy in the final dish. Add the black-eyed peas, stock, and ham hock, and incorporate thoroughly. Simmer for 1 hour or until thickened and black-eyed peas are tender.

Makes 3 quarts.

TIP:
THIS RECIPE IS ALSO GREAT IF YOU SUBSTITUTE RED BEANS FOR BLACK-EYED PEAS. IF YOU DON'T HAVE A HAM HOCK OR DON'T HAVE TIME TO PREPARE YOUR OWN STOCK, SUBSTITUTE PREPARED CHICKEN STOCK IN PLACE OF THE WATER.

CAJUN JAMBALAYA

It's hard to find a festival or fundraiser in South Louisiana where jambalaya isn't the most anticipated dish. My cousins, my siblings, and I were all in 4-H from age nine to age 18. We raised hogs and sheep—although my dad did 90 percent of the work and paid for all of the actual raising of the animals. We won many awards throughout the years with our show animals because of his hard work, and we got to keep the proceeds from the sale of the animals as our spending money for the year. Our family couldn't afford much, so we made the most of the yearly district and state livestock shows in Covington and Baton Rouge and treated the time away from school as a vacation.

At the annual district livestock show, Billy and Joan Lasseigne and Paul and Evelie Scioneaux would make huge pots of delicious Cajun jambalaya and white beans to sell to raise money for the St. James High School Future Farmers of America. They started cooking long before we arrived at 6:00 A.M. I know it was a lot of work, but you could see the pride they took in it and the joy it brought them to cook for everyone.

1 large onion, diced	½ link Wayne Jacob's andouille,
2 bunches green onions, chopped	quartered and sliced
1 head celery, diced	1 lb. ground pork
3 green bell peppers, seeded and diced	1 bay leaf
1 tbsp. chopped garlic	3 tbsp. Worcestershire sauce
¼ cup canola oil	6 tbsp. Circle Z Seasoning Mix (see Index)
1 lb. pork, diced	1 quart chicken stock
2 links Wayne Jacob's Smoked	1 quart beef stock
Sausage, sliced	4 cups rice, washed thoroughly

In a large Dutch oven over medium heat, sauté chopped onion, green onions, celery, peppers, and garlic in oil until translucent and starting to brown. Mix in next seven ingredients and cook until browned, stirring often to prevent sticking. Add half of each stock to deglaze the pot. Simmer uncovered over medium heat until all meat is fully cooked and most of the liquid has cooked out. Add remaining stock and simmer for 30 minutes uncovered. Check seasoning. The dish should be strongly seasoned to account for the additional liquid and rice to be added. Mix in rice and 4 cups water, stirring to make sure the rice doesn't stick to the bottom of the pot. Liquid should just cover all of the ingredients. Allow the mixture to return to a simmer and then cover the pot and reduce heat to low. Cook covered for 20 minutes. Remove from heat but allow the dish to rest and do not open the pot for 10 minutes. This will allow any uncooked rice to finish steaming. Remove lid, stir, and serve.

Makes 8 quarts.

STUFFED VENISON ROAST

White-tailed deer hunting is a popular tradition in Vacherie and throughout South Louisiana. When hunting any animal, Cajuns kill only what they will eat and use every part of the animal that they can. Venison roast is one of the prized pieces from a deer. Although venison is a very lean meat, if prepared right it will melt in your mouth. I serve this with white beans and Louisiana rice.

1 venison roast
6 cloves whole garlic
2 tsp. salt
2 tsp. black pepper
½ tsp. cayenne pepper
4 tbsp. flour, divided
3 tbsp. canola oil
1 onion, thinly sliced
2 tbsp. Worcestershire sauce
1 quart homemade deer stock or
   beef stock

Preheat oven to 350 degrees. Clean roast of all connective tissue. Cut slits into each side of roast and insert whole garlic cloves. Season roast with salt, black pepper, and cayenne pepper and dust with 1 tbsp. flour. Heat oil in a braising pot over high heat. Brown roast on all sides then remove from pot and set aside. Add remaining flour to the pot and cook, stirring constantly to make a roux that is caramel in color. Add sliced onion to roux and cook until caramelized. Deglaze the pot with Worcestershire sauce and stock, stirring to release all of the browned bits, or fond, from the bottom of the pot. Return the roast to the pot and cover. Place in oven and cook for about 90 minutes, until roast is fork tender. Slice and serve with the gravy from the pot.

Serves 4

CAULIFLOWER GRATIN

With the Keto diet craze and gluten allergies, cauliflower seems to be the go-to substitute for many foods. Everything from rice to pizza crusts to steaks and burgers have cauliflower as the star impersonator. This is because the flavor of cauliflower is easily masked with seasonings and its texture lends well to different treatment.

My dad always says that he loves to grow a winter garden because he just plants it and it grows. He grows cauliflower and cabbage the size of basketballs, broccoli that produces all winter, and turnips and beets by the truckload.

2 heads cauliflower (about 8 cups)
2 cups diced onions
3 cloves garlic, chopped
1 cup fresh parsley
1 cup butter
1 tbsp. Circle Z Seasoning Mix
  (see Index)

2 tbsp. cornstarch or flour
½ cup dry white wine
2 cups half-and-half
1 cup grated Parmesan cheese

Preheat oven to 425 degrees. Arrange cauliflower in an oven safe baking dish and set aside. In a large pan over medium heat, sauté onions, garlic, and parsley in butter until translucent. Mix in seasonings and cornstarch, stirring constantly until the mixture thickens. Deglaze with wine. Add half-and-half and Parmesan cheese. Stir until thickened. Pour mixture over cauliflower and bake for 30 minutes.

Serves 6.

PARMESAN MASHED TURNIPS

Turnips are very easy to grow; you can just scatter the seeds and ignore them. The less attention you pay to them, the better they do. With my harvest, I usually make a beef and turnip stew, but one day I was thinking about the earthy flavor of turnips and realized that Parmesan cheese would be a great complement. This is a full-flavored side for any meat or fish and an alternative use for the incredibly easy-to-grow turnip.

8 cups turnips, peeled and cubed
2 tsp. salt
¼ cup butter
½ cup grated Parmesan cheese
½ cup heavy cream

Boil turnips until fork tender and drain well. Transfer boiled turnips to a mixing bowl, mash them, and whisk in salt, butter, Parmesan cheese, and cream.

Serves 6.

Residents of Edgard, Louisiana, on the banks of a frozen Mississippi River in 1899.
Courtesy of the Collections of the Louisiana State Museum, 1998.001.16.036

SLOW COOKER (OR NOT) GRILLADES

Mardi Gras is the time of year when we Louisianans reconnect with our love of this place. All over the state people go all-out to celebrate before Lent. Each region has its own traditions, krewes, costuming, and parades.

From the time my siblings and I were very young, my parents would take us to the parades in Metairie. No matter the weather, we were out there with ice chests, insulated camouflage onesies, blankets, and of course the ladder. One year we saw Louise Mandrell on the Sanderson Farms chicken float.

Our parade-watching accommodations improved once my brother and I moved to New Orleans. Our landlord and friend, Carlos, would throw a huge party for the Bacchus parade. Complete with a huge spread of food, a brass band, unlimited liquor, and old and new friends, we were based just a few blocks away from the parade route. With the beer keg in a shopping cart, the entire party would migrate to the parade. We carried on this tradition until Hurricane Katrina, when many of our lives took different directions.

We always begin Fat Tuesday by blaring "Mardi Gras Mambo" to wake the house. This is not a drill; it is an all-day marathon. I cook many things for Mardi Gras day but either fried chicken, jambalaya, gumbo, or grits and grillades are guaranteed to be on the menu—something warm and filling that we can return to all day. I prep the grillades the night before and put the whole pot in the oven or the slow cooker first thing on Mardi Gras Day.

TO PREPARE THE GRILLADES IN A SLOW COOKER, ADD ALL INGREDIENTS IN ORDER TO THE COOKER. COOK ON HIGH SETTING FOR 6-8 HOURS OR UNTIL THE BEEF FALLS APART. SERVE OVER GRITS (SEE INDEX FOR PERFECT GRITS).

1 cup oil or bacon fat
1 cup flour
3 lb. beef roast (chuck or sirloin tip works great) or pork butt, cut into 4-6 inch pieces
2 cups diced onions
1 cup diced celery
1 cup diced bell pepper

1 cup sliced green onions
6 oz. canned tomato paste
28 oz. canned diced tomatoes
2 tbsp. Worcestershire sauce
1 quart beef stock
4 tbsp. Circle Z Seasoning Mix (see Index)

Preheat oven to 350 degrees. In a Dutch oven, prepare the roux by whisking together oil and flour over medium heat, stirring constantly until roux is the color of caramel. Add the roast, cut into pieces, to brown in the roux. To that mixture, add the onions, celery, bell pepper, and green onions. Stir often to prevent sticking. When the vegetables are wilted and translucent, add tomato paste, diced tomatoes, Worcestershire sauce, beef stock, and seasonings. When the mixture returns to a boil, cover and transfer the pot to the preheated oven and cook for 3 hours or until the beef falls apart. Serve over grits (see Index for Perfect Grits).

Makes 6 quarts.

SMOKED RABBIT CASSOULET AND COLLARD GREENS

Smoked rabbit cassoulet is a dish that sounds hard but is actually easy to make. It requires only 30 minutes of prep time and the oven does the rest. A great one-pot meal for a cold evening, it contains two of my favorite things: white beans and smoked meat. You can serve it as a soup with French bread, with Louisiana grown rice, or with a side of roasted vegetables.

Stock

1 Wayne Jacob's smoked rabbit, quartered
1 unpeeled onion, quartered
2 tbsp. black peppercorns
1 tbsp. salt
1 bay leaf
Trimmings from cassoulet vegetables

Cassoulet

¼ lb. cubed bacon or 6 slices bacon, chopped
½ cup butter
1 cup flour
2 cups diced onions
2 cups diced celery
2 cups chopped green onions
4 cups chopped leeks
4 cups sliced carrots
12 garlic cloves, peeled
¼ cup Circle Z Seasoning Mix (see Index)
½ cup brandy
1 lb. white beans
1 bunch parsley, chopped

To make the stock, in a large pot boil rabbit in 6 quarts water for 10 minutes. Remove rabbit from water and set aside to cool. De-bone the rabbit, reserving the meat, and return bones to the pot. Add quartered onion, peppercorns, salt, bay leaf, and vegetable trimmings from the cassoulet to the stock. Return to a boil, allowing the stock to reduce to about 4 quarts.

Meanwhile, prepare the cassoulet. In a Dutch oven over medium heat, render bacon until crispy. Remove bacon from the pot and set aside. Add butter and flour to bacon fat, stirring constantly to make a roux about the color of peanut butter. Mix in onions, celery, green onions, leeks, carrots, garlic cloves, seasoning mix, and brandy and cook until onions and leeks are caramelized. Add white beans and 4 quarts stock. Cover and bake at 350 degrees for 3 hours. Stir in chopped parsley after removing from the oven.

Serves 8.

COLLARD GREENS WITH SMOKED PORK BELLY

Growing up, we ate collard greens every once in a while, but my family preferred mustard greens and turnip greens because they were more delicate and, more importantly, we were already growing turnips. Collard greens take a bit more love and work than other greens. The stems have to be removed from fresh collards and since they are thicker, they have to be cooked a bit longer. To me the reward is definitely worth the extra effort.

2 cups cubed smoked bacon
4 cups diced onions
3 lb. fresh collard greens, stemmed and chopped
2 tbsp. Circle Z Seasoning Mix (see Index)

In a large pot, render bacon until crispy. Remove from pot and set aside. Sauté diced onions in bacon fat until translucent. Add collard greens, bacon, seasoning mix, and 2 cups water to prevent sticking. Cover and cook over medium heat until greens are tender, about 30 minutes.

Serves 6.

KEKS

Cultures all over the world have recipes for fried breads. They go by different names, and the most famous version we have locally is a beignet. We referred to the ones we made at home as "keks."

My grandmother, Anabell Shexnayder Zeringue, made these for us anytime we would spend the night at her house. We knew we were in for a treat when we'd awaken to the smell of keks frying in her black iron skillet. My father now makes them for us every Christmas morning. We spread butter over them and drizzle them with cane syrup.

2 cups flour
1½ tsp. baking powder
1½ tsp. salt
1 cup buttermilk
Oil for frying

In a stand mixer and using a dough hook, combine flour, baking powder, salt, and buttermilk. Mix on low for 8 minutes. Do not cut this time short as the gluten must develop in the dough in order for it to puff when fried. When ready, dough should form a ball around the hook. Remove dough to a floured surface and flatten to ¼-inch thickness. Cut into rectangles measuring approximately 2x6 inches. Cut a slit in the middle of each. Drop individually into deep fryer and fry until golden brown. Serve with whipped butter on top and a side of cane syrup or homemade jam.

Makes about 30 keks.

TIP:
TASSO QUESO SAUCE IS ALSO GREAT AS AN APPETIZER DIP WITH CHIPS OR PORK RINDS.

BOUDIN BREAKFAST STACK

Each week for brunch at Wayne Jacob's Smokehouse, we experiment with fun specials. We generally feature one Benedict-style stacked dish, one over-the-top sweet dish, and one egg dish.

One of my favorite stacked dishes involves boudin. Boudin in South Louisiana is one of those humble items that you can find not only at gas stations (and often these are the best-tasting), but also on some of the fanciest menus in the state. It is a mixture of ground pork, liver, rice, and seasonings stuffed into a pork casing. It can be steamed, grilled, or smoked.

4 boudin links

Remove boudin from the casing and shape into patties. Pan-fry over medium-high heat until outer edges become crisp. Stack them onto a Drop Cracklin Biscuit (see Index) split in half and top with poached eggs and hollandaise or my Tasso Queso Sauce.

Serves 4

Tasso Queso Sauce
¼ cup butter
¼ cup flour
1 bunch green onions, chopped
¼ cup chopped Wayne Jacob's tasso
2 cups milk
4 cups granted pepper Jack cheese

In a 2 quart saucepan over medium heat, whisk together butter and flour. Cook, stirring constantly, until roux just begins to caramelize. Add green onions and tasso and fry in roux for about 5 minutes to release the smoke flavor from the tasso. Whisk in milk to incorporate completely. Add cheese and whisk until smooth and thickened. Use as a dip or topping for breakfast, potatoes, or pasta.

Makes 2 quarts.

DROP CRACKLIN BISCUITS WITH STEEN'S BUTTER

Once a year on the day after the boucherie, my mom would chop up the fresh cracklins and add them to her drop biscuit dough. The fat on the small pieces would melt into the dough, leaving the little chunks of meat to stud the biscuit. With a little Steen's Butter and a hot cup of coffee we had the perfect breakfast. You can enjoy our cracklin biscuits with Steen's Butter at Wayne Jacob's Smokehouse ever Sunday for brunch.

4 cups all-purpose flour
1 tbsp. sugar
2 tbsp. baking powder
1 tbsp. baking soda
½ tsp. salt
1 cup cracklin crumbs
½ cup cold butter
1½ cups buttermilk

Preheat oven to 425 degrees. In a large bowl sift together flour, sugar, baking powder, baking soda, and salt. Mix in cracklin crumbs. Grate cold butter into flour and mix well to distribute the butter. Stir in buttermilk. Using an ice cream scoop, space biscuits evenly on baking sheet, leaving room for them to rise in the oven. Bake for 20 minutes or until golden. Serve with Steen's Butter or homemade jam.

Makes 24 biscuits.

Steen's Butter
½ cup butter, softened
¼ cup Steen's cane syrup

Whisk together butter and syrup. Spread on warm biscuits. Leftovers can be refrigerated.

Makes approximately ¾ cup.

BETTY BOO'S BREAD PUDDING

Uncle Lewis was Mama Winnie's brother, and Aunt Betty was his wife. They were wonderful people. He doted on her and they loved being together. He was a big man and she was a short lady. Both were kind, thoughtful, and loving. Aunt Betty was a worrier and whatever Uncle Lewis could do to make her happy and content, he would do. He was an amazing carpenter and a great cook, and he learned both skills from his father.

I have a few of my aunt and uncle's recipes, including a hand-written copy of their bread pudding recipe. Just like gumbo, there are no two bread budding recipes that are the same. Theirs is the basis for the bread pudding I make at my restaurants because I like the lighter texture. Mama Bell added meringue and bananas to hers, but I bake a simpler version that we top with a whiskey sauce.

1½ loaves stale French bread, torn into 1-inch pieces	8 oz. jar maraschino cherries
8 cups whole milk	2 tbsp. cherry juice
3 cups evaporated milk	2 cups raisins
1½ cups room temperature butter	1 tbsp. vanilla extract
1¾ cups sugar	1 tbsp. butternut extract
6 eggs	1 tbsp. pineapple extract
28 oz. canned crushed pineapple	1 tbsp. banana extract
	1 tbsp. lemon extract

Preheat oven to 350 degrees. Arrange French bread in a 9x13 baking dish. Cover with milk and evaporated milk and set aside. In a mixing bowl, cream together butter and sugar until fluffy, then mix in eggs one at a time. Pour over bread. Combine remaining ingredients and then mix into the French bread mixture, incorporating thoroughly. Bake about 1 hour or until puffed and set. Serve with Whiskey Sauce.

Serves 16.

Whiskey Sauce

4½ cups brown sugar
1 cup whiskey
1 lb. butter
4 eggs, beaten

In a saucepan, melt butter and sugar over medium heat. Remove from heat and stir in whiskey to fully incorporate. Whisk in eggs until sauce is thickened.

Makes approximately 5 cups.

ANABELL'S T-GATEAU

Mama Bell would make these iced cookies after Thanksgiving, and we would eat them throughout the holiday season. I still remember playing with the cookie cutters she used. They probably once belonged to her mother and most likely dated from the 1920s. There were farm animals and other shapes, all made of tin. She would make hundreds of these cookies and ice each and every one with pastel icing.

Cookies
1 cup butter
1⅓ cups sugar
2 eggs
½ tsp. salt
1 tsp. vanilla
3 cups flour
½ tsp. baking soda

Royal Icing
3½ cups confectioners' sugar
2 egg whites
2 tbsp. milk

Preheat oven to 325 degrees. In a stand mixer fitted with a flat beater, cream butter and sugar together on medium speed until fluffy then add eggs one at a time. Add remaining ingredients and mix to incorporate. Transfer dough to a floured board and shape into a ball. Wrap with plastic wrap and move to refrigerator to cool. Chill for an hour in the refrigerator, and then roll out on a floured board to about ¼-inch thickness. Cut with cookie cutters and place on a cookie sheet lined with parchment paper. Bake for 8-10 minutes or until lightly browned.

To make royal icing, beat confectioners' sugar and egg whites in a stand mixer with whisk attachment until tripled in volume. Slowly add milk to achieve desired thickness. Add food coloring as desired. Royal icing may be spread or piped onto cooled cookies and will harden as it dries.

Makes 4 dozen cookies.

100 GOOD COOKIES

These cookies are addictive. That's a good thing because this recipe will actually make 100! I recommend keeping them small so they bake to be light and crispy.

1 cup sugar
1 cup rice cereal
1 cup quick oats
1 cup canola oil
1 egg
1 cup brown sugar
1 cup coconut
1 cup butter
3½ cups flour
1 tsp. vanilla
1 tsp. baking soda
1 tsp. cream of tartar
¾ tsp. salt

Preheat oven to 350 degrees. In a large bowl, combine all ingredients, mixing well. Drop dough by teaspoonfuls onto ungreased cookie sheet. Bake for 10-15 minutes. When done, cookies will be golden with slightly browned edges.

Makes 100 cookies.

CHRISTMAS ROCKS

My mom and dad bake these cookies every year for the holidays. This recipe, like the other recipes in this chapter, makes a lot of cookies. These Christmas Rocks are great to give as gifts, but the spices in them will overpower the flavors of other cookies so be sure to keep them in a separate tin or bag.

3½ cups flour
1½ cups sugar
3 eggs
¾ cup butter
1 tsp. cinnamon
½ tsp. allspice
1 tsp. baking soda dissolved in
  1 tbsp. water
1½ lbs. pecans, chopped
1 cup chopped dates or raisins

Preheat oven to 325 degrees. In a large bowl, combine all ingredients, mixing well. Drop dough by tablespoonfuls onto a lined baking sheet. Bake for 20 minutes until edges are golden.

Makes 4 dozen cookies.

DELICIOUS FRUITCAKE

Each of my mom's two brothers has a special fruitcake recipe, but one of them makes his extra special by soaking his cake in whiskey. Here I've taken my grandmother's recipe, added a few updates, and worked that whiskey into the baking process. Add more to soak if you like!

I use two bowls to make this recipe so that the fruit can macerate in the juice and liquor without activating the baking soda and baking powder prematurely.

Bowl 1

½ lb. butter (2 sticks)
4 eggs
¼ cup molasses
1 tsp. vanilla
1 orange, zested and juiced

1 lemon, zested and juiced
2 tsp. lemon extract
1 cup bourbon
¼ cup sherry
2 cups brown sugar

Bowl 2

1½ cups pecans, coarsely chopped
1 lb. dates, coarsely chopped
1 cup sliced almonds
3 cups golden raisins
1 cup dried cherries
2 cups dried apricots
3 cups flour

1 tsp. baking powder
1 tsp. baking soda
½ tsp. salt
1 tsp. nutmeg
½ tsp. cloves
2 tsp. cinnamon

In Bowl 1, whisk together the butter and wet ingredients. Mix in brown sugar and set aside.

In Bowl 2, toss pecans, dates, almonds, and fruit with flour, baking powder, baking soda, salt, and spices.

Preheat oven to 275 degrees. Butter and line two 9-inch round pans or one 9x13 baking pan. Pour dry mixture in Bowl 2 over the wet mixture in Bowl 1. Mix just until incorporated. Do not overmix. Pour into pans and immediately transfer to oven. Place a pan of water at the bottom of the oven and bake cakes for 2-3 hours. Check with a toothpick for doneness.

Makes 2 9-inch cakes or 1 9x13 cake.

CHOCOLATE CAKE 5 WAYS

This is the best and easiest chocolate cake recipe. I've used it for about 20 years. When I make it at the restaurants, I mix several batches of the dry ingredients and store the extras for later. When it is time to make the cake, I just pull out one of the dry mixes, add the remaining wet ingredients, and bake. With all of the different ways to finish a chocolate cake, you will have trouble repeating the same one.

Chocolate Cake

1¾ cups flour
2 cups sugar
¾ cup cocoa powder
2 tsp. baking soda
1 tsp. baking powder
1 tsp. salt

1 cup buttermilk
1 tsp. vanilla extract
1 cup coffee
½ cup vegetable oil
2 eggs

Preheat oven to 350 degrees. In a large mixing bowl, sift together dry ingredients. In a separate bowl, combine wet ingredients and whisk until eggs and oil are incorporated. Add wet mixture to dry and stir until just combined. Do not overmix. Pour into two 9-inch lined and greased pans and bake for 30 minutes or until set and toothpick comes out clean. You will start to see the edges of the cake separating from the sides of the pan when done. Run a knife around the edge of the pan and allow to cool for at least 10 minutes before turning out onto parchment or a cooling rack. Layers must be completely cooled before icing.

Serves 12.

Chocolate Icing

6 oz. semisweet chocolate
1 cup butter, room temperature
1 egg yolk
1 tsp. vanilla
1¼ cups confectioners' sugar

Melt chocolate in a double boiler over medium heat, then remove from heat and allow to cool. In a stand mixer with a whisk attachment, cream butter with confectioners' sugar. Add egg yolk and vanilla and beat on low. Add cooled melted chocolate and beat on high until fluffy.

German Chocolate Icing

1½ cups sugar
¾ cup butter, melted
1½ cups evaporated milk
6 egg yolks
1½ cups coconut
1½ cups chopped toasted pecans
2 tsp. vanilla extract

In a saucepan over medium heat, whisk together sugar, melted butter, evaporated milk, and egg yolks, stirring constantly until thickened. Remove from heat and fold in coconut, pecans, and vanilla. Allow to cool before icing cake layers.

Chocolate Ganache

1½ cups heavy cream
3 tbsp. butter
24 oz. semisweet chocolate chips

Combine all ingredients in a double boiler over medium heat. Heat until smooth and shiny, stirring occasionally. Do not let steam from the double boiler near the chocolate as it may cause it to seize up or curdle. Allow ganache to cool to room temperature before pouring over chilled cake layers. Smooth with an offset spatula.

Whipped Ganache Frosting

1½ cups heavy cream
3 tbsp. butter
24 oz. semisweet chocolate chips

Combine all ingredients in a double boiler over medium heat. Heat until smooth and shiny, stirring occasionally. Do not let steam from the double boiler near the chocolate as it may cause it to seize up or curdle. Allow ganache to cool to room temperature then add cooled ganache to a stand mixer. Using a whisk attachment, beat on high until ganache is light and fluffy with stiff peaks.

Chocolate Fudge Icing

2 cups sugar
2 tbsp. cocoa powder
1 cup evaporated milk
½ cup butter

Combine all ingredients in a saucepan over medium heat. Heat until mixture begins to separate from the bottom of the pot when stirred (similar to the hard ball stage). Remove from heat and beat by hand until mixture begins to thicken. Spread on cake immediately.

DIVINITY FUDGE

Candy making centers around the temperature of sugar. For fudge and pralines, the sugar will have to reach 240 degrees, or the "soft ball" stage, meaning that if you put a drop of the sugar mixture into cold water it will form a malleable ball. The higher the temperature you cook the sugar, the harder that ball will be when dropped into cold water. Popcorn balls require a "hard ball" stage—260 degrees—to achieve the sticky consistency. For sugar sculpting and brittle candies, the sugar must reach 300 degrees, or the "hard crack" stage. The temperature to which you heat your sugar mixture will dictate your final product.

When making candy with sugar it is also important to work in a dry environment or even better, on a dry day. When there is too much humidity in the air, the sugar can seize up and crystallize too quickly or not set up at all.

3 cups sugar
½ cup water
¾ cup light Karo syrup
3 egg whites
⅛ tsp. salt
1 tsp. vanilla
1 cup pecans

In a heavy saucepan over medium heat, combine sugar, water, and syrup. Stir to dissolve sugar and bring to a boil. Boil over medium heat until the temperature reaches 240 degrees, or the soft ball stage. Meanwhile, beat egg whites and salt in a stand mixer until the egg whites form stiff peaks. Slowly pour the hot syrup into the egg whites while the mixer is running at a medium speed. Beat the mixture for about 5 minutes, until it loses its shine. Either stir in pecan pieces and spoon by the tablespoonful onto waxed paper, or spoon out and immediately top with a pecan half. Work quickly as the fudge will set as it cools.

Makes 24 pieces.

SPRING

Spring in South Louisiana brings crawfish, river shrimp, potatoes, blackberries, onions, garlic, shallots, strawberries, and green onions.

The trees are budding, and the grass is growing and green again. The snow melt in the north is causing the Mississippi River to rise while we hold our collective breath until after it peaks in May. From the ships passing on the river, we can tell that the water is definitely higher than our heads. It is a true testament to our trust in the Army Corps of Engineers, the same folks who were responsible for the flooding of New Orleans after Hurricane Katrina in 2005. But there are more important things to be concerned with. This is the season for river shrimp and crawfish. When the Mississippi River floods, we throw shrimp boxes and fishing lines in its waters to see what we can catch. That deeply engrained sense of making the most of what is given is in all of us.

It is also time to plant summer gardens. The general rule is to plant tomatoes after March 8. By this time, we should be past any morning frosts or freezes. Potatoes that were planted in the fall are ready for harvest. Across the sugarcane fields, the ditches are lined with blackberry bushes. There are a few spots that we have left to grow undisturbed over the years. These spots can yield as many berries as we can pick to make jam, wine, and cobblers. The onions and garlic are ready now as well. Strawberries are celebrated on every restaurant menu and with a huge festival in the town of Ponchatoula. In Chackbay, fields of shallots—in this area the green onion and the shallot are considered one and the same—line the route from Vacherie to Thibodaux. Such bounty is reflected in our festivities and in our meals.

CRAWFISH BOULETTES WITH REMOULADE

When I was a child, my grandmothers, Winnie and Annabell, dropped these boulettes into stews. I've also had them pan-fried and smashed between two pieces of Bunny Bread. Today I serve these as an appetizer. I use the same stuffing to stuff the crawfish heads for my Easter Sunday Crawfish Bisque (see Index).

Oil for frying
2 cups corn flour for dredging
2 tbsp. Circle Z Seasoning Mix, divided
1 lb. Louisiana crawfish tails, chopped
⅓ cup finely chopped onion
⅓ cup finely chopped green onions
½ cup breadcrumbs
1 tbsp. Worcestershire sauce
⅓ cup buttermilk
1 egg

Fill a deep fryer to the maximum fill line with oil. Preheat oil to 350 degrees. While oil is heating, combine corn flour and 1 tbsp. seasoning mix in a shallow bowl. In a mixing bowl, combine remaining ingredients. By the tablespoonful, shape stuffing into balls, dredge in corn flour, and fry in deep fryer. Serve hot with Remoulade.

Makes about 20 boulettes.

Remoulade
½ cup olive oil
¼ cup Creole mustard
¼ cup red wine vinegar
2 tbsp. lemon juice
1 stalk celery, chopped
2 tbsp. paprika
1 tbsp. horseradish
2 tsp. chopped garlic
2 tsp. black pepper
2 cups chopped green onions
5 dashes Tabasco

For the remoulade, combine all ingredients in a deep bowl. Blend with immersion blender and refrigerate until ready to serve.

Makes 1 quart.

ANDOUILLE CHEESECAKE

This delicious, savory cheesecake can be served warm or cold. It is perfect for parties and can be made into bite-size hors d'oeuvres as well.

½ cup butter
½ link Wayne Jacob's andouille, casing removed, and sliced
1 leek, chopped and washed
1 red pepper, seeded and diced
16 oz. cream cheese
⅔ cup mayonnaise
3 eggs
2 tbsp. Creole mustard
1 tsp. salt
1 tsp. black pepper
2 tbsp. biscuit mix

Crust
1¼ cups Italian breadcrumbs
½ cup grated Parmesan cheese
3 tbsp. butter
½ cup pecan pieces
3 dashes Tabasco

Melt butter in a large pan over medium heat. Sauté andouille, leek, and red pepper. In a stand mixer, combine cream cheese, mayonnaise, eggs, mustard, salt, pepper, and biscuit mix. Add andouille mixture to cheese mixture and mix well to incorporate.

In a separate bowl or food processor, combine all crust ingredients. Press crust into greased 9 inch springform pan and bake at 350 degrees for 10 minutes. Pour andouille and cream cheese mixture into crust and bake at 350 degrees for 1 hour or until set. Remove from oven and let rest for at least 30 minutes before removing the spring form mold.

Serves 12.

ANDOUILLE

Andouille is a smoked sausage that was originally brought to Louisiana from France in the 1700s. When the Acadians settled in the River Parishes outside of New Orleans, they mingled with the German settlers who had first made the area their own. Although they were living on *la Côte des Allemands*, or the German Coast, French became the language of business and French tastes soon began to influence the local cuisine. The Germans had brought their own traditional sausages and smoked meats from their homeland, but their neighbors were French so they adapted their sausage for their new customers. Thus the andouille of Louisiana's River Parishes is a German sausage with French influences and a French name.

Traditionally andouille was made from organ meats and other remnants so as not to waste any part of the animal. Over the years, changing tastes, mechanization, and an expanding market have led producers to standardize the cuts of meat and the production process. However, andouille is still made by hand, and there are marked differences between local products.

BRUSSELS SPROUT SALAD 3 WAYS
(AND NONE OF THEM ARE BOILED)

Like many other things, ingredients come into and go out of fashion. Recently, the Brussels sprout has been having its moment. In the 1980s we only saw these boiled or steamed, and they were pretty gross. Now chefs and home cooks have learned what to do with them and they are hot.

Hot Roasted Brussels Sprouts

1 lb. Brussels sprouts
2 cups cherry or grape tomatoes
½ onion, sliced

3 tbsp. olive oil
1 tbsp. apple cider vinegar
2 tbsp. Circle Z Seasoning Mix (see Index)

Preheat oven to 425 degrees. Clean and cut stems from Brussels sprouts. Halve the Brussels sprouts, saving any loose leaves. Toss with tomatoes, sliced onion, olive oil, apple cider vinegar, and seasoning mix. Roast in a single layer on a sheet pan for 20 minutes.

Serves 4.

Brussels Sprout Slaw

1 lb. Brussels sprouts, thinly sliced
1 roasted red pepper, thinly sliced
¼ cup Parmesan cheese
½ red onion, thinly sliced
3 tbsp. olive oil

1 lemon, juiced and zested
2 tbsp. red wine vinegar
½ cup chopped pecans
1 tsp. salt
1 tsp. black pepper

Combine Brussels sprouts, roasted red pepper, Parmesan cheese, and red onion. Toss with olive oil, lemon juice and zest, and red wine vinegar to coat. Mix in pecans and season with salt and black pepper.

Serves 6

Fried Brussels Sprouts with Bacon Vinaigrette

Oil for frying
1 lb. Brussels sprouts
6 slices Wayne Jacob's bacon, chopped

3 tbsp. goat cheese
¼ red onion, sliced
3 eggs, boiled, peeled, and chopped

Fill a deep fryer to the maximum fill line with oil. Preheat oil to 350 degrees. Clean and cut stem from Brussels sprouts. Halve the Brussels sprouts, saving any loose leaves. Deep fry until the edges start to turn golden. Remove from the oil and immediately toss with Bacon Vinaigrette, bacon, goat cheese, red onion, and chopped boiled eggs.

Serves 4.

Bacon Vinaigrette

½ cup bacon grease
3 tbsp. Creole mustard
3 tbsp. apple cider vinegar
½ shallot, chopped
1 tsp. black pepper
1 tsp. kosher salt

Whisk ingredients together in a bowl. Toss thoroughly with fried Brussels sprout mixture. Serve warm.

Makes approximately 1 cup.

GERMAN POTATO SALAD

This is a great potato salad to go with smoked meats or barbecue. The bacon, vinegar, and horseradish give it substance and a complex flavor.

2 lb. red potatoes, quartered
6 slices Wayne Jacob's smoked bacon, chopped
4 boiled eggs, peeled and chopped
1 bunch green onions, chopped
3 oz. sour cream
1 tbsp. Creole mustard
1 tsp. horseradish
2 tbsp. red wine vinegar
1 tsp. black pepper
1 tsp. salt

In a large pot, boil quartered red potatoes until fork tender. Meanwhile, in a pot over medium heat, add chopped smoked bacon and water to cover. Being careful not to burn the bacon, heat until the water has cooked out and the bacon begins to get crispy and the fat begins to foam. In a large bowl, mix eggs, green onions, sour cream, Creole mustard, horseradish, and vinegar. Fold in hot potatoes and bacon, including the bacon fat, and mix together. Season with salt and pepper. Serve warm or cold.

Serves 6.

POTATO AND SAUSAGE STEW

This one-pot meal is one of my favorite comfort dishes. I remember as a young child picking red potatoes for my grandfather in what seemed like a huge field. On the day of harvest, neighbors would come to help. Everyone would take as many as they could use throughout the year. The rest would be delivered to others in the community. My grandfather would store the potatoes he kept for his own use in a huge wooden box in the darkest and coolest corner of his shed.

1 cup canola oil
1 cup all-purpose flour
1 large onion, diced
1 bunch green onions, sliced
1 bunch Italian parsley, chopped
3 cloves garlic, chopped
1 lb. Wayne Jacob's smoked sausage, sliced
2 tbsp. Worcestershire sauce
4 tbsp. Circle Z Seasoning Mix (see Index)
1 lb. red potatoes, diced
1 chicken bouillon cube

In an 8 quart Dutch oven, heat canola oil over medium heat. Add flour to make a roux, stirring constantly until the roux is medium brown. Add onion, green onions, parsley, garlic, sausage, Worcestershire sauce, and seasoning mix. Sauté in roux until onions are translucent and sausage starts to render. Add potatoes, bouillon cube, and just enough water to cover the ingredients. Cover pot and cook on low about 30 minutes until potatoes are tender, stirring often. Serve over rice.

Serves 6.

TIP:
THIS IS A GREAT RECIPE FOR TURNIP STEW IF YOU SUBSTITUTE TURNIPS FOR POTATOES. SHRIMP ALSO WORK WELL AS A SUBSTITUTE FOR SMOKED SAUSAGE.

PAPA PHILIP'S CHICKEN STEW

My grandfather, Philip Eloi Chauvin, Jr., is one of my heroes. A farmer, Korean War veteran, and lightning strike survivor, he walked away from many car crashes, beat encephalitis, and outlasted 20 years in a nursing home. He was an escape artist and lover of food, cigarettes, liquor, and running the road. He was the proud father of four, grandfather of nine, and a great-grandfather many times over.

His life journey with my grandmother Winnie is difficult to believe. To his last day, the commitment they had for each other is inspiring. He was the taste tester for Grandmother's amazing cooking, and my grandmother's chicken stew was my grandfather's favorite thing to eat. The best compliment he would give was a nod then say it was "alright." Even though he wasn't able to eat toward the end, I am confident that if given the choice, he would have eaten her chicken stew with his last breath.

1 cup canola oil, divided
1 whole fryer hen, cut into pieces
1 cup all-purpose flour
1 large yellow onion, diced
1 bunch green onions, chopped
1 cup chopped Italian flat leaf parsley
2 cloves garlic, minced
2 tbsp. salt
1 tbsp. black pepper
1 tsp. cayenne pepper
2 tbsp. Worcestershire
8 cups hot water

In a Dutch oven over medium heat, brown chicken pieces in a ¼ cup canola oil. Remove browned chicken from pot and set aside. Add remaining oil and flour to make a roux, stirring constantly until the roux is a medium brown the color of crawfish fat. Sauté diced onion, green onions, parsley, and garlic in roux. Mix in seasonings to incorporate. Add hot water and simmer, covered, until chicken has fallen off of the bones and the stew is thickened, about 3 hours.

Serves 6.

TIP:
THIS STEW MAY BE COOKED ON EITHER THE STOVETOP OR IN THE OVEN.

CRAWFISH BOIL STEW

This is a great one-pot meal for a cool spring day. It contains all the great ingredients of a crawfish boil without the hassle of having to peel the crawfish.

2 sticks butter
1 cup all-purpose flour
1 large onion, diced
1 bunch green onions, sliced
4 stalks celery, diced
1 green bell pepper, seeded
  and diced
1 bunch Italian parsley, chopped
8 whole cloves garlic, peeled
3 lb. Louisiana crawfish tails
1 lb. red potatoes, diced
3 ears fresh sweet corn, cut
  into rounds
1 tbsp. granular Zatarain's Crab Boil or
  Old Bay Seasoning
1 tbsp. Worcestershire sauce
2 tbsp. Circle Z Seasoning Mix
  (see Index)
4 quarts chicken stock
8 eggs, boiled and peeled

Melt butter in an 8 quart Dutch oven over medium heat. Add flour to make a roux, stirring constantly until the roux is a medium brown color. Sauté onion, green onions, celery, bell pepper, parsley, garlic, and crawfish tails in roux until onions are translucent, about 15 minutes. Add potatoes, corn, crab boil, Worcestershire sauce, seasoning mix, and chicken stock. Cover pot and simmer 30-40 minutes, until potatoes are tender and corn is cooked, stirring often. Add boiled eggs to the stew or garnish each bowl with half an egg. Serve over rice.

Serves 8.

GOOD FRIDAY DINNER CRÊPES

Good Friday is the last Friday in Lent. In the Catholic faith it is the day that Jesus was crucified. In South Louisiana this is traditionally a very solemn day. The observant shall not eat meat, they are not to dig in the ground, and they are to fast. However, in New Orleans, Good Friday is the busiest day of the year for restaurants with seafood on their menus. So much for fasting.

As an altar boy at St. Philip Catholic Church, Good Friday meant that I had to serve for the Stations of the Cross, the symbolic reenactment of the Passion of Christ. It was a long service. The reward was that afterward my mom would make crêpes for dinner. No filling or anything fancy, just simple crêpes with sugar and butter. This is not to say that we didn't participate in the seafood feasts other Fridays in Lent, but we looked forward to this Good Friday tradition.

4 eggs
2⅓ cups milk
1 tsp. vanilla extract
⅔ cup sugar
2⅓ cups all-purpose flour
½ tsp. kosher salt
4 tbsp. butter, melted

In a mixing bowl, whisk together all ingredients and chill in the refrigerator for 1 hour. Heat a very clean nonstick skillet over medium-low heat. Lightly grease the pan before your first crêpe. Ladle ¼ cup of batter onto the pan and swirl to evenly cover the entire surface. Heat 30 seconds to 1 minute, depending on the heat and thickness of the pan. When the edges of the crêpe start to curl up, gently shake the pan. The crêpe will release from the surface when it is time to flip. Flip to cook the other side for about 20 seconds. The first one probably won't be the prettiest, but this recipe makes 20, so you'll get the hang of it. Top with sugar and butter or fill with your favorite fruits, chocolate, or caramel. To make savory filled crêpes, just eliminate the sugar and vanilla.

Makes 20.

THIS IS A LARGE RECIPE BUT FOR THE AMOUNT OF TIME AND EFFORT INVOLVED, PLAN TO INVITE PEOPLE OVER OR SAVE SOME IN THE FREEZER FOR LATER. IT IS JUST AS GOOD OR BETTER OUT OF THE FREEZER.

EASTER SUNDAY CRAWFISH BISQUE

During my childhood, I never went without crawfish bisque on Easter Sunday. Even today, I can't recall a year in which this dish was not served. One year my family even travelled 13 hours by train to Atlanta, and Mama Winnie brought all the fixings to make the bisque at our destination. She would spend days leading up to Easter Sunday scrubbing crawfish heads, chopping seasoning, stuffing heads, frying heads, and making the bisque. It was, and still is, time consuming and can seem overwhelming. But it is worth every bit.

Each year we stuff 1,200 heads and make 25 gallons to serve at my restaurants from Good Friday through Easter Sunday. This dish is one that transports people back to their childhoods in their mother's or grandmother's kitchens. It definitely takes me back.

Stuffed Heads

2 lb. Louisiana crawfish tails with fat, peeled
1 cup chopped onions
⅓ cup chopped green onions
1 cup chopped celery
1 cup chopped green bell peppers
3 cloves garlic, chopped
¼ cup chopped parsley
¾ cup buttermilk
5 eggs, separated
8 slices white bread
2 tbsp. salt
1 tsp. red pepper
100 crawfish heads, cleaned
4 cups flour for dredging

Bisque

1 cup butter
1 cup canola oil
2 cups flour
2 cups diced onions
1 cup finely chopped green onions
2 cups diced celery
3 lb. Louisiana crawfish tails with fat
2 tbsp. Circle Z Seasoning Mix (see Index)
2 tbsp. Worcestershire sauce
¼ cup seafood base
1 cup chopped parsley

For the stuffed heads, finely chop the crawfish tails. In a large bowl, mix chopped crawfish tails with onions, green onions, celery, green peppers, garlic, and parsley. In a separate bowl, pour buttermilk and egg yolks over sliced bread. After the bread has absorbed the milk and eggs, stir with a fork. Pour bread mixture into the crawfish mixture and season with salt and red pepper. Mix thoroughly. Spoon into a piping bag and pipe into crawfish heads. After filling heads, dip each into egg whites and then dredge in flour. Line dredged crawfish heads on a baking sheet and bake at 350 degrees for 20 minutes.

In a 20 quart stockpot over medium heat, melt butter. Stir in oil and add flour to make a roux, stirring constantly until the roux is the color of peanut butter. Sauté diced onions, green onions, and celery in the roux, stirring constantly until onions are translucent. Add crawfish tails and fat, seasoning mix, Worcestershire sauce, and 5 quarts water. Bring to a simmer, making sure to deglaze the bottom of the pot. Simmer covered for 30 minutes then add fresh parsley and stuffed crawfish heads. Simmer for another 30 minutes. Taste to check seasonings. Serve over rice.

Serves 20

TIP:

YOU CAN SUBSTITUTE
BONELESS LOIN CHOPS
POUNDED THIN INSTEAD OF
BONE-IN, THIN-CUT CHOPS.

PANÉED PORK CHOPS

This was one of my mom's weeknight meals, served with a side of smothered green beans, mashed potatoes, or her favorite, red beans. My mom was a teacher for 20 years and then went back to school to become a nurse. No matter how busy she was, she always had a hot dinner on the table no later than 5:00 PM. I usually "helped" by bringing her slippers to her, because she hadn't made it as far as her room before she busied herself cooking. Measured against the standard she set, I am definitely doing life wrong.

2 tbsp. Circle Z Seasoning Mix
   (see Index)
6 thin-cut, bone-in pork chops
2 eggs, beaten
3 cups Italian breadcrumbs
2 tbsp. oil

Sprinkle the seasoning mix on the chops. Dredge in the beaten eggs and then in the breadcrumbs. In a frying pan over medium heat, brown the porkchops in the oil, being careful not to overcrowd the pan. When the porkchops are golden on both sides, remove and drain on a wire rack or on paper towels. The wire rack will keep them crispy.

Serves 6.

SMOTHERED GREEN BEANS

In late spring the green beans are ready to pick. They are so plentiful that we "snap" them and freeze them to use throughout the year. One dish we prepare with the bounty is smothered green beans. Although most cultures appreciate the crunch of fresh beans, Cajuns smother them down with potatoes and cured pork.

1 large onion, chopped
1 clove garlic, chopped
1 lb. cured pork such as ham, tasso, andouille,
   or salt pork, cubed
¼ cup butter
5 lb. fresh green beans, cleaned
1 lb. red potatoes, quartered
1 tbsp. salt
1 tbsp. black pepper

In a Dutch oven over medium heat, sauté onion, garlic, and pork in butter until caramelization begins, about 20 minutes. Fold in green beans and potatoes. Season with salt and pepper. Deglaze pot with 4 cups water and cover to simmer. Cook approximately 30 minutes, until potatoes are tender and water is cooked out.

Serves 6.

TARTE À LA BOUILLE

I remember my great-grandmother, Esperance Leroux Chauvin, baking these when I was a small child. I was a little scared of my great-grandparents because they were so old, but they would give us each a dollar when we'd visit. Sometimes we would also get a stuffed mirliton or a piece of this delicious pie.

Filling
¾ cup flour
¾ cup sugar
2 eggs
2 cups whole milk
12 oz. canned evaporated milk
¼ cup butter, cubed
1 tbsp. vanilla extract

Sweet Dough Pie Crust
1 sticks butter
¾ cup sugar
1 egg
1 tbsp. vanilla extract
2 cups flour (plus more as necessary)
1½ tbsp. baking powder

For the filling, mix together flour and sugar in a large mixing bowl. Add eggs and mix well. Set aside. In a large saucepan, bring milk and evaporated milk to a boil. Stir flour mixture into the milk, whisking until it thickens. Remove from the heat and stir in cold butter and vanilla until completely incorporated. Set aside to cool.

Meanwhile, make the crust. In a stand mixer on medium speed and using the flat beater attachment, cream together butter and sugar. Add egg and vanilla, mixing well to incorporate. Add flour and baking powder and incorporate thoroughly. If dough is too wet, add more flour to achieve a crumbly texture that holds together when squeezed.

Divide dough into 4 pieces. Roll out 2 pieces and place into 2 buttered pie pans. Trim excess dough. Pour the cooled custard into the unbaked pie dough. Roll out the remaining 2 pieces and cut strips for the lattice topping. Arrange dough into a lattice across the custard. Bake at 375 degrees for about 30 minutes, until the center is almost set and the lattice is golden.

Makes 2 8-inch pies or 1 12-inch tart.

BUTTERMILK PIE

David Smith is the reason I decided to take the step into the restaurant business. Having been raised in his family's St. Francisville restaurant, South of the Border, he was eager to open a restaurant in New Orleans. About three months after Hurricane Katrina, we were talking about a vacant building in the French Quarter. Over dinner that night, we had a couple bottles of wine and decided to put a business plan together to submit to the building's owner. During the next decade, David continued to guide me through the opening of more restaurants.

This is his mother's Buttermilk Pie recipe, which has been a very popular menu item at my restaurants.

9-inch pie crust
1 cup sugar
4 eggs
½ cup butter, melted
1 cup buttermilk
1 tsp. vanilla extract
3 tbsp. biscuit mix
Optional toppings of your choice, such as
   almonds, coconut, or chocolate chips

Bake prepared pie crust for 10 minutes at 350 degrees. In a bowl, mix sugar, eggs, melted butter, buttermilk, vanilla, and biscuit mix. Pour into pie crust. Add sliced almonds and amaretto, coconut, or chocolate chips. Bake until the middle is set.

Makes 1 pie.

BLACKBERRY CRISP

Blackberries grow wild behind the levee, along the ditches of the cane fields, and along any road in the River Parishes. They are very abundant but the season is short. We make desserts, jam, and wine with them.

6 cups fresh blackberries, washed
2 oranges, zested and juiced
1 cup dark brown sugar
1 tbsp. cinnamon
3 tbsp. flour

Topping
1 cup flour
½ cup dark brown sugar
¼ cup butter
½ cup chopped pecans

Preheat oven to 350 degrees. Arrange blackberries in a 9x9 pan. In a small bowl, whisk orange juice, zest, brown sugar, cinnamon, and flour together and pour over blackberries. In a separate bowl, mix the topping ingredients together by hand until a crumbly mixture forms. Sprinkle over the blackberries. Bake for 30 minutes or until brown and bubbly. Remove from oven and let stand for at least 20 minutes to set. Serve warm with vanilla ice cream.

Serves 6.

STONE FRUIT TART WITH PECAN SHORTBREAD CRUST

I love ripe peaches, plums, pears, cherries, and apples, but it is becoming harder and harder to find great stone fruit in grocery stores. They are usually rock hard or tasteless because they have to be picked before they are ripe to ship across the country or the world. Fortunately, cooking unripe fruit will release and develop flavors that you will not get eating them fresh.

Crust

1 cup finely chopped pecans
2 cups flour
½ tsp. kosher salt
½ tsp. baking powder
1 cup butter at room temperature
½ cup sugar
2 tsp. vanilla extract

Filling

8 cups fresh fruit of your choice
3 tbsp. cornstarch
3 tbsp. sugar
½ cup apricot jam

Preheat oven to 350 degrees. For the crust, mix all ingredients together and press into the bottom and sides of a 12-inch tart pan. Refrigerate about 30 minutes then prepare the filling.

To make the filling, toss fruit with cornstarch and sugar in a mixing bowl. Arrange fruit onto the crust. Heat the apricot jam. With a pastry brush, apply the apricot jam to cover the fruit. Bake for 1 hour at 350 degrees.

Makes 1 12-inch tart.

JELLY ROLL

Any time there was a bake sale at our elementary school in Thibodaux, my grandmother was the hit of the school. We would give Mama Bell a week's notice and she would make a few trays of these for us to sell. I found out years later that all of the teachers would take shifts watching each other's classes so they could get the sweets from Vacherie before everything had been picked over. I guess that explains why the only jelly roll I ever saw was when I dropped the tray off in the morning.

Batter
6 eggs
1½ cups sugar
¾ cup cake flour
¾ cup all-purpose flour
1½ tsp. baking powder
Pinch of salt
1½ tsp. vanilla extract

Pecan Filling
1 cup evaporated milk
1 cup sugar
3 egg yolks
¼ cup butter
1 tsp. vanilla extract
1 cup chopped pecans, toasted

To make the batter, in a stand mixer, beat eggs until very fluffy (about 5 minutes, no joke), then gradually add sugar. In a separate bowl, mix cake flour, all-purpose flour, baking powder, and salt. Gradually incorporate flour mixture into egg and sugar, then add vanilla. Do not overmix.

Preheat oven to 350 degrees. Grease 2 jelly roll pans liberally. Line each pan with a greased sheet of waxed paper. Divide batter evenly onto pans and spread to the edges. Bake about 10 minutes, until done but not brown.

While the cake bakes, prepare the filling. Combine all filling ingredients, except pecans, in a saucepan over low heat. Cook mixture for 12 minutes, stirring often, until mixture darkens and thickens. Stir in pecans and beat until thick. Remove from heat and set aside.

Lay 2 towels out and sprinkle them with sugar. Turn hot jelly rolls onto towels and remove waxed paper. Carefully roll cake and towel from the narrow end. Allow cake to cool completely. Unroll cake and remove towel then spread cake with filling. Roll cake and wrap in waxed paper.

Makes 2 jelly rolls.

OTHER FILLING FLAVORS

Caramel

In a large pot, completely submerge in boiling water 1 unopened 12-ounce can of condensed milk. Boil for 3 hours. *Warning*: Do not let the water evaporate or it will explode!

Strawberry

Use a good quality store-bought jam.

Lemon Condensed Milk

Mix together 1 12-ounce can of condensed milk, the zest of 1 lemon, ½ cup of fresh squeezed lemon juice, and 2 egg yolks.

TIP:

THE INITIAL ADDITION OF THE ¼ CUP OF FLOUR WILL KEEP THE WET MIXTURE FROM BREAKING, THUS PREVENTING A DENSE CAKE.

HEAVENLY HASH CAKE

Easter Sunday as a kid was almost as exciting as Christmas. We always awoke to a basket full of candy. Most of the candy was Elmer's brand, a local institution since 1855 and today made in Ponchatoula, Louisiana. The Pecan Egg, the Gold Brick Egg, and the Heavenly Hash Egg were always included amongst the plastic green grass and the malted eggs that we would lick before painting our lips with the candy coating. Inspired by the Elmer's candy, Mama Bell would make Heavenly Hash Cake for Easter Sunday. It has all of the ingredients of the chocolate-and-marshmallow egg but it is better by far.

Cake

1 cup butter
2 cups sugar
1½ cups self-rising flour, divided
1 tsp. vanilla
4 eggs
2 tbsp. cocoa powder
2 cups chopped pecans

Icing

4 tsp. cocoa
½ cup butter, room temperature
3¼ cups confectioners' sugar
8 tsp. heavy cream
1 bag miniature marshmallows

Preheat oven to 375 degrees. In a stand mixer, cream butter and sugar together. Add ¼ cup flour and vanilla and mix to incorporate. Add eggs one at a time, beating well between each addition. In a separate bowl, mix cocoa, remaining flour, and pecans. Add dry mixture to wet mixture and fold in just to incorporate. Do not overmix. Bake in a greased 9x13 pan for 30 minutes or until a toothpick comes out clean when inserted into the middle of the cake. Remove from oven and allow to cool before icing.

For the icing, whisk together cocoa, butter, powdered sugar, and heavy cream until smooth. Fold in marshmallows and spread over cooled cake. Divide cake into even squares.

Makes 18 pieces.

NANAINE ANNE'S FRUIT SALAD

Although my Nanaine Anne used some canned fruit—as I'm sure was all the rage when she first began to make this ambrosia-style salad—the fresh fruit version is just as good if not better. Other seasonal or favorite fruits can be substituted but keep in mind that the shelf life of some cut fruits is very short.

4 oz. cream cheese, room temperature
2 cups confectioners' sugar
½ pineapple, peeled, cored, and cubed
2 cups halved grapes
1 pint strawberries, quartered
1 pint blackberries
2 peaches, sliced
2 cups orange supremes or mandarin slices
10 oz. miniature marshmallows

In a large mixing bowl, whisk or use a hand mixer to incorporate cream cheese and confectioners' sugar until smooth. Fold in the prepared fruit and marshmallows. Serve chilled.

Serves 8.

SUMMER

A South Louisiana summer brings okra, Creole tomatoes, sweet peppers, eggplant, squash, zucchini, watermelon, muscadines, figs, cantaloupe, shrimp, and crabs.

As a kid there was no explaining the excitement I felt this time of year. I hated school and this was my break from it. In the summer we spent every afternoon at the pool for swim team and hanging with friends. I wish I still had that time every year to relax. Now it's processing food shipments in 90-degree heat, cutting trees for firewood while soaked in sweat, cooking in kitchens that never cool off, and working in itchy gardens. It seems that every summer crop has itchy leaves.

Okra have to be picked every day and served fresh or they will be too tough to eat. Creole tomatoes are so plentiful that I have to tie the limbs so they don't break. Bell peppers are so fragrant that they will perfume your house. Ripe eggplant, squash, and zucchini hide from the sun under the canopy of their leaves. Watermelon and cantaloupe vines cover the ground for meters. (I hope the raccoons leave a few for us this year.) Muscadines and figs, rarely seen fresh in grocery stores, are ripe. Their incredibly short season requires us to be vigilant. When the trucks start appearing on the side of the road advertising fresh shrimp and crabs, we will find a reason to celebrate.

TASSO BAKED EGGS

These eggs are a simple and delicious breakfast, perfect for dipping broiled buttered French bread. Serve them with a side of Wayne Jacob's bacon.

3 tbsp. chopped Wayne Jacob's tasso
¼ cup butter
3 green onions, sliced
3 tbsp. chopped Italian parsley
2 tsp. salt
2 tsp. black pepper
¼ tsp thyme
1 cup heavy cream
8 eggs
¼ cup Italian breadcrumbs mixed
  with 2 tbsp. melted butter
French bread, sliced and buttered.

Set oven to broil. In a heavy oven-safe skillet over medium heat, sauté diced tasso in butter with green onions, parsley, salt, black pepper, and thyme. Stir in heavy cream and when large bubbles form, add eggs. Remove from heat and top with breadcrumb mixture. Transfer skillet to oven, and broil until breadcrumbs are browned. Remove from oven and set aside to cool; the residual heat will continue to cook the eggs. Meanwhile, broil the buttered French bread. Serve eggs with French bread on the side for dipping in yolks and tasso cream.

Serves 4

SPICY DEVILED EGGS

The key to making fluffy, creamy deviled eggs is a food processor or a hand mixer. A whisk just doesn't get the same volume. Volume is important to me because I always seem to run out of filling and have egg white halves left unstuffed. I like a little kick to my deviled eggs as well.

1 dozen eggs, boiled and peeled
1 tbsp. Creole mustard
2 tbsp. mayonnaise
1 tbsp. dill relish
1 tbsp. chopped pickled jalapeño plus
    more for garnish
½ tsp. black pepper
5 dashes hot sauce
Crumbled bacon for garnish (optional)

Slice eggs in half lengthwise. Being careful not to break the whites, separate whites from yolks and transfer to separate bowls. Mash the yolks with a fork and combine with the rest of the ingredients. Mix with an immersion blender or hand mixer until fluffy and smooth. Scoop yolk filling into egg white halves or fill a piping bag with a star tip for a nicer presentation. Garnish with a sliced jalapeño or a piece of bacon.

Makes 24 deviled eggs.

FRIED VEGETABLE PLATTER

We went out to eat at family-style restaurants pretty often, but rarely to any place that was fancy and expensive. There were a few times in my childhood when I got to experience a really nice restaurant. Either I had tagged along on adult day or it was a very special occasion. One of the places that captured this magic for me as a kid was Flanagan's in Thibodaux. There were parts of the menu that were so pricey I wasn't even allowed to look at them. But it was also a place that exposed me to many classic, upscale South Louisiana dishes.

Whatever we ordered was always preceded by a fried vegetable platter. This platter would feature fried onion rings, pepper rings, green beans, okra, eggplant, squash, and zucchini—all perfectly golden and seasoned with ranch dressing of course. I always enjoyed the appetizer but found its presence curious, mainly because we grew the same vegetables on that plate but I never seem to remember us frying them at home. We always cooked our garden vegetables in the same ways. Maybe we didn't think our homegrown stuff was ready for primetime.

4 cups canola oil
1 egg yolk
2 cups buttermilk
3 cups flour
½ cup cornstarch
2 tbsp. kosher salt
2 tbsp. black pepper
1 onion, cut into rings

1 bell pepper, cut into rings
12 fresh green beans
12 okra, cut from stem to tip
1 small eggplant, cut into rounds or sticks and salted
1 yellow squash, cut into sticks
1 zucchini cut, into sticks

In a Dutch oven heat oil to about 325 degrees. While oil is heating, whisk together buttermilk and egg yolk in a mixing bowl. In a separate bowl mix flour, cornstarch, salt, and pepper. Dip vegetables one by one into the wet mixture then into the dry mixture. One at a time, carefully place each piece in the hot oil. If too many pieces are fried at a time, you may end up with a mess of tangled vegetables stuck to each other. Because frying times vary between vegetables, fry each type of vegetable separately. When golden, remove vegetables from oil and place on a paper-lined tray or rack to drain. Lightly salt while hot and eat with your favorite dipping sauce.

Serves 6.

CRAB GRATIN

My mom made crab gratin for many special occasions. Served with buttered and toasted French bread, it is a decadent appetizer. I use a mixture of claw and lump crabmeat in this recipe because the claw is more flavorful and the lump is more indulgent. Be sure to fold in the crabmeat carefully so as not to break it up too much.

½ lb. butter
1 cup diced onions
1½ cups chopped green onions
2 tbsp. Circle Z Seasoning Mix (see Index)
½ cup flour
½ cup vermouth
1 quart half-and-half
1 cup grated Parmesan cheese
1 lb. backfin or lump crabmeat
1 lb. claw crabmeat
2 tsp. granulated crab boil

Breadcrumb Topping
1 cup grated Parmesan cheese
1 cup Italian breadcrumbs
½ cup melted butter

Melt butter in a large oven-safe skillet over medium heat. Sauté onions and green onions in butter until translucent. Add seasoning mix and flour, stirring constantly. Deglaze with vermouth. Add half-and-half and Parmesan cheese. Stir until thickened. Fold in crabmeat and set aside to cool while you prepare the breadcrumb topping.

In a mixing bowl, combine Parmesan cheese, breadcrumbs, and melted butter to make the topping. Sprinkle over crabmeat and broil until golden. Serve with sliced, buttered, and toasted French bread.

Makes 2½ quarts.

WAYNE JACOB'S SMOKED CHICKEN SALAD

Most of the smoked chicken we sell at Wayne Jacob's Smokehouse is for use in our customers' chicken and andouille gumbo, but during the summer, when it is just too warm to eat a hot meal, our smoked chicken is perfect for a unique chicken salad. I like to add grapes, pecans, and celery for texture.

1 Wayne Jacob's smoked chicken
½ cup finely diced celery
¼ cup chopped green onions
2 cups halved red seedless grapes
3 boiled eggs, chopped
½ cup chopped pecans
¾ cup mayonnaise
1 tbsp. Creole mustard
1 tbsp. Circle Z Seasoning Mix (see Index)
3 tbsp. red wine vinegar

De-bone the chicken and chop the meat. Combine all ingredients in a mixing bowl and fold to incorporate. Eat as a sandwich, as a salad over a spring mix, or with crackers.

Makes 3 quarts.

I MAKE A SMOKED POBLANO
VINEGAR AT WAYNE JACOB'S,
SOLD IN OUR ONLINE STORE,
THAT IS THE PERFECT WAY TO
FINISH THIS SUMMER SALAD.

WATERMELON AND CORN SALAD

Watermelon and corn are big summer crops. On their own, they are delicious eaten fresh, straight out of the garden, but they also complement each other well. A little acid and salt balance the sweetness.

4 cups chopped seedless watermelon
3 cups Creole tomato slices
1 ear fresh corn, cut from the cob
¼ cup red onion, thinly sliced
¼ cup feta cheese
4 cups baby arugula
2 tbsp. white vinegar or Wayne Jacob's
   Smoked Poblano Vinegar
3 tbsp. olive oil
Freshly ground black pepper to taste

Combine watermelon, Creole tomato, fresh corn, red onion, feta cheese, and baby arugula. Drizzle with vinegar and oil. Season with freshly ground black pepper.

Serves 4.

WARM OKRA AND TOMATO SALAD

Most people around here eat okra smothered, cooked in gumbo, or fried. Okra is also delicious roasted.

1 lb. okra, sliced lengthwise (from stem to tip)
3 tbsp. olive oil
1 tbsp. salt
1 tbsp. black pepper
2 cups grape tomatoes
½ cup goat cheese
¼ lb. Wayne Jacob's bacon
½ cup pecans

Lemon Shallot Vinaigrette

1 shallot, chopped
1 tbsp. Dijon mustard
1 lemon, juiced and zested
1 tsp. salt
1 tsp. black pepper
½ cup olive oil

Preheat oven to 425 degrees. Toss okra with olive oil, salt, and black pepper. Arrange in an oven-safe pan or black iron skillet and roast in oven for 15 minutes. While okra is roasting, whisk together all vinaigrette ingredients except oil. Whisk in oil to emulsify then set aside. Remove roasted okra from the oven and top with grape tomatoes, goat cheese, bacon, pecans, and lemons shallot vinaigrette. Return to the oven and roast for another 5 minutes. Serve warm.

Serves 4.

CREOLE TOMATO, CHADRON, AND CUCUMBER SALAD

The summer is all about Creole tomatoes. They are the star of any summer garden and rightfully so. A ripe Creole tomato, when sliced, can be smelled from across the kitchen. No grocery store tomato can claim that. Although there is actually a breed of Creole tomatoes, I've read that as long as the tomato grows in the sandy soil of the Mississippi River, it qualifies for the label. I believe the soil has a great deal to do with the superiority of taste, and that the tomatoes get to ripen in the hot Louisiana sun is probably an important part of the equation.

As kids, my cousin Andre and I were banished from the house in the summer from sunup to sundown, and we had to find ways to entertain ourselves. Besides building forts in trees and riding bikes, we would also catch crawfish, pick blackberries, and cut down "chadron." A chadron is the stalk of a thistle—those plants with the big purple flower on the end. The entire plant is covered in serious thorns, but the stalk is edible. Of course, we would look for the largest ones to conquer, but the smaller ones were actually more tender and flavorful.

2 Creole tomatoes, cut into
  bite-size pieces
1 quart chadron (thistle stalk), peeled
  and cut into bite-size pieces
2 cucumbers, sliced

Creole Vinaigrette
1 clove garlic, chopped
1 tbsp. Creole mustard
3 tbsp. white vinegar
1 egg yolk
1 tsp. salt
1 tsp. black pepper
½ cup olive oil

In a serving bowl, combine tomatoes, chadron, and cucumbers. In a small bowl, whisk together all vinaigrette ingredients except oil. Whisk in oil to emulsify. Dress tomatoes, chadron, and cucumbers with Creole vinaigrette and serve.

Serves 4.

TIP:
ADD A LITTLE CREAM OR FRESH HERBS FOR ADDED FLAVOR.

ROASTED CREOLE TOMATO SOUP

For a couple of weeks in the early summer we are blessed with Creole tomatoes. Each year, both experienced farmers and novice gardeners plant way too many tomato plants after the last frost. My mother and father tend separate tomato gardens side by side. My father's garden is more traditional while my mother prefers heirloom varieties. Ferrol "Coco" Keating, nephew of Mr. Nolan Jacob, founder of Wayne Jacob's Smokehouse, sells his tomatoes across from the smokehouse under a tent with a hand-painted sign. He sells only the best from his more than 600 plants, and he sometimes gives me a few of the ugly ones to make sauce. His mother Hilda Jacob Keating worked seasonally as a butcher at the store, and we still keep her photo on the wall.

These incredibly fragrant and tasty tomatoes are extremely abundant for this short time, filling market counters and populating roadside stands for a few weeks. This soup is very easy to make and a great way to ensure that none of your harvest goes to waste. I make many seasonal vegetable soups with this method and each is a hit.

12 Creole tomatoes, quartered
2 large yellow onions, quartered
1 red pepper, quartered and seeded
6 cloves whole garlic
3 tbsp. olive oil plus more for garnish
1 tbsp. kosher salt
1 tbsp. black pepper
Pinch red pepper flakes

1 tsp. thyme
6-inch stale French bread, broken
    into pieces
2 quarts chicken stock
Croutons to garnish (optional)
Goat cheese to garnish (optional)
Basil to garnish (optional)

Preheat oven to 425 degrees. In a large bowl, toss tomatoes, onions, red pepper, and garlic cloves with olive oil, salt, black pepper, red pepper flakes, and thyme. Arrange tomato mixture on a sheet pan and roast in oven for 25 minutes. Transfer roasted vegetables, including any juices from the pan, to an 8 quart pot. To the roasted vegetables, add French bread and chicken stock. Bring to a simmer and cook for 20 minutes. The French bread will thicken and add body to the soup. Puree the soup and serve with croutons, a little olive oil, a spoon of goat cheese, and fresh basil, or use it to dip your favorite grilled cheese sandwich.

SERVES 6

COCO'S CREOLE TOMATOES
985-652-9786

OKRA AND SHRIMP GUMBO

In New Orleans, the Creole style of seafood gumbo usually has okra, shrimp, crab, and oysters. In the River Parishes we have okra and shrimp gumbo and then we have seafood gumbo (with no okra). I'll say it again: no two gumbos are alike. However, there are lines that shouldn't be crossed. These lines are forever the point of contention amongst gumbo makers.

Okra grows like a weed in the hot summer months of South Louisiana. It has to be picked every day or it will grow too large and woody to be of any use. The plant is prickly and itchy, which makes it that much more fun to pick while dripping sweat.

When my mom was young, she and her cousins would drop shrimp boxes into the Mississippi River to catch river shrimp. Since they were so poor, she would bring her catch to the seamstress down the road who would make dresses in exchange for the shrimp.

3 lb. okra, sliced
2 lb. 60/70 Louisiana shrimp, peeled; reserve shells and heads
1 cup canola oil
1 large yellow onion, quartered
2 bay leaves
1 tbsp. granular Zatarain's Crab Boil
1 cup flour
2 large yellow onions, diced

1 head celery, diced
2 green bell peppers, diced
2 bunches green onions, chopped
3 cloves garlic, minced
1 bunch Italian parsley
4 tbsp. Circle Z Seasoning Mix (see Index)
3 tbsp. Worcestershire sauce
28 oz. diced tomatoes, drained

Preheat oven to 350 degrees. In an oven-safe dish, cook okra for 1 hour, covered, stirring twice. Meanwhile, in a 10 quart pot over medium heat combine shrimp peelings and oil. Fry shrimp peelings in the oil until bright orange and fragrant. Transfer peelings to a 4 quart pot, add quartered onion, 3 quarts water, bay leaves, and crab boil to make a rich stock. Simmer over medium heat while preparing the roux mixture.

To the oil in the 10 quart pot add flour to make a roux. Cook over medium heat, stirring constantly until the roux is caramel colored. Add diced onions, celery, peppers, green onions, garlic, and parsley to roux. Stir to combine. Add seasoning mix and Worcestershire sauce. The salt in the seasonings will help to draw moisture from the vegetables. They will cook faster and the spices will bloom in the oil. Cook until onions are translucent.

Incorporate tomatoes, smothered okra, and shrimp stock to roux. Bring to a simmer. Cook for 30 minutes. Add shrimp and cook, partially covered, over low heat for 30 minutes, stirring occasionally. Serve over rice.

Makes 6 quarts.

BUTTERBEANS WITH SHRIMP

   This one-pot meal is a staple in the River Parishes. I made a batch at one of my New Orleans restaurants as a special and word spread like wildfire. It has been our best-selling dish over the years. Mama Winnie and my mother both have this recipe on their short list.

1 cup butter
1¼ cups flour
2 cups diced onions
1 cup chopped green onions
2 lbs. frozen (or 1 lb. dry) butterbeans
   or baby lima beans
3 tbsp. Worcestershire sauce
1 bunch Italian parsley, chopped
3 tbsp. Circle Z Seasoning Mix
   (see Index)
1 quart chicken stock
2 lb. 60/70 shrimp, peeled

   Melt butter in an 8 quart pot over medium heat. Add flour, stirring constantly to make a medium-dark roux the color of caramel. Add onions and green onions, and sauté in roux until the onions are translucent. Mix in beans, Worcestershire sauce, parsley, seasoning mix, and chicken stock. Add 1 quart water and simmer until beans are tender and creamy, about 30 minutes. Stir in the shrimp and cook for another 20 minutes, until shrimp are pink and curled.

Serves 6.

BARBECUE SHRIMP

Pascale's Manale Restaurant, opened in 1913, is credited with the invention of New Orleans-style barbecue shrimp. For my own restaurants, I have devised my own recipe to pay homage to their legendary dish. Tourists are sometimes disappointed when there is no actual "barbecue" sauce on the shrimp, and others try to bribe the waiters to peel the shrimp for them.

5 lb. 21/25 or larger Louisiana shrimp
   with shells and heads on
5 tbsp. Circle Z Seasoning Mix
   (see Index)
2 tbsp. chili powder
2 tbsp. paprika
½ cup Worcestershire sauce
½ cup lemon juice
¼ cup chopped garlic
2 cups butter
1 loaf French bread, sliced

Do not peal shrimp or remove their heads, as the dish will be more flavorful if the shell remains intact

Preheat oven to 350 degrees. Rinse shrimp and arrange in a baking dish. In a separate bowl, combine next 6 ingredients and pour over shrimp. Slice butter and arrange over the seasoned shrimp. Cover with foil and bake for 30 minutes, stirring once halfway through. When done, shrimp should be curled and orange in color, and the shell should be separating from the meat. Serve with fresh French bread and plenty of napkins.

Serves 4

Locals fishing on the water's edge, 1890s. Courtesy of the Collections of the Louisiana State Museum, 1998.001.16.032

FRIED FISH

Just as we had barbecues for holidays and gatherings, we also had fish fries. My Papa Rene used to set fish traps in Lake Des Allemands and in the surrounding bayous. My parrain, Donald Chauvin, would take me fishing around Bayou Chevreuil and Bayou Gauche, where we would catch perch and sac-a-lait, the white crappie. Sometimes we would just park the truck on the side of Bayou Chevreuil Road and fish from the bank.

Oil for frying
4 lb. fish fillets (I prefer perch,
    sac-a-lait, or catfish)
2 cups buttermilk
3 tbsp. Creole mustard
3 tbsp. Circle Z Seasoning Mix
    (see Index)
3 cups cornmeal

Heat oil in a heavy frying pan to about 350 degrees. Mix buttermilk and Creole mustard to form the wet batter. In a separate bowl, mix seasoning mix with cornmeal for the dry batter. Dredge each fish fillet in the wet batter then in the dry batter. Place battered fish in hot oil and fry until golden.

Serves 6.

TIP:
THE CRAB STUFFING ALSO
SERVES AS A GREAT RECIPE
FOR CRAB CAKES.

When I was a child, stuffed flounder was one of the dishes I would see on menus at fancy restaurants in South Louisiana. I considered that dish to be the epitome of luxury. I mean, you can't get any better than seafood-stuffed seafood. When we opened Vacherie Restaurant in 2013, I knew I had to have it on the menu.

This is one of those showstopper dishes that can be daunting but isn't very hard. Flounder, like red snapper, is a very versatile, mild, flaky, and delicious fish that is often cooked whole. The skin of each is thin and not very oily. The fish vary in size so you can cook smaller flounder for individual servings or cook a larger one as a centerpiece to share. As always when eating whole fish, be careful as bones can be a choking hazard.

2 lb. whole flounder or ½ lb. small
   flounder per person
1 tsp. salt
1 tsp. black pepper
1 cup white wine
1 cup lemon juice

Crab Stuffing

1 lb. Louisiana crab claw meat
1 lb. Louisiana lump crabmeat
¼ cup Creole mustard
½ cup mayonnaise
2 tsp. kosher salt
2 tsp. black pepper
1 egg
1 lemon, zested and juiced
1 tbsp. Worcestershire sauce
5 dashes Tabasco
2 cups Italian breadcrumbs

Sauce

1 shallot, chopped
Salt to taste
Black pepper to taste
2 tbsp. cold butter

Lay flounder on a cutting board. From below the gill to just before the tail, make a slit down the center of the fish to the depth of the rib cage. With a fillet knife, carefully free the flesh from both sides of the rib cage. Remove the rib cage, being careful not to cut the fillets too much in the process. There should be a nice cavity, free of bones, in the flounder to stuff. Set aside while making the stuffing.

Preheat oven to 350 degrees. Turn crabmeat out into a bowl to check for shell pieces, being careful not to break the meat up. In a separate bowl, whisk together the rest of the ingredients except for the breadcrumbs. Carefully fold mixture into crabmeat. Fold in breadcrumbs. Open the flounder to stuff it with the crab mixture, at least ½ cup of stuffing per person. The flesh of the fish will be overstuffed and hold the fillets apart. This will also allow steam to escape while cooking.

Transfer flounder to a baking dish. Sprinkle with salt, black pepper, white wine, lemon juice, and 1 cup water. Bake until crab stuffing reaches an internal temperature of 165 degrees. The skin should begin to loosen from the fish when done.

To make a sauce, transfer the poaching liquid to a pan over high heat. Add chopped shallot and salt and pepper to taste. Reduce liquid by half, remove from heat, and whisk in cold butter. Drizzle over stuffed flounder.

Serves 4.

Shrimp & Crab - stuffed Flounder

1½ lbs. - uncooked shrimp

10 T. butter, cut into ½" bits, plus 3 T. butter melted.

1½ cups soft fresh crumbs made from French or
   Italian-type white bread; pulverized in a blender

⅓ cup finely chopped onions

⅓ cup finely chopped green peppers

⅓ cup finely chopped celery

⅓ cup finely chopped scallions including 3 inches of the gree

2 t. finely chopped garlic

⅓ cup finely chopped drained canned tomatoes

4 t. Worcestershire sauce

1½ t. Creole mustard

½ t. ground hot red pepper

2 t. salt

1 lb. (2 cups) fresh, frozen, or canned crabmeat, thoroughly draine
   picked over to remove all bits of shell or cartilage

3 T. finely chopped fresh parsley preferably _____ leaf to

Four 1½ lb. flounders, cleaned with the heads removed
   the tails intact

¼ t. freshly ground black pepper

Shell the shrimp. Devein them by making a shallow incision dow
backs with a small sharp knife and lifting out the black or white
vein with the point of the knife. Wash the shrimp briefly in a c
et under cold running water.

IF YOU WANT TO CUT THE
RECIPE IN HALF, CONSIDER
ELIMINATING ONE OF THE
SEAFOOD CHOICES SINCE
THEY ARE MOSTLY SOLD BY THE
POUND.

SEAFOOD FETTUCCINE

My family still loves to tell the story of me as a child sitting down at restaurants and ordering whatever I wanted, no matter the price. They tell the tale as if it were my intention to bankrupt the family. I guess no one had explained to me that we couldn't exactly afford many of the items on the menu. My dad claims that he actually would count the money in his wallet as I was ordering to make sure we had enough. We didn't eat out often, but when there was something to celebrate, we always marked the occasion with a delicious meal. Once I realized that there were limits to how much money was in my father's wallet, I settled on seafood fettuccine as my go-to dish at Politz's Restaurant in Thibodaux, Louisiana. I remember the huge chunks of local sweet crab claw meat and shrimp, tossed with fettuccine in a garlicky alfredo sauce. It was probably enough for two meals but I never left a trace in the bowl.

½ cup butter	½ tsp. cayenne pepper
1 onion, diced	½ cup flour
3 stalks celery, diced	4 cups whole milk
1 green bell pepper, seeded and diced	½ cup heavy cream
3 cloves garlic, chopped	1 cup grated Parmesan cheese
2 tbsp. Worcestershire sauce	1 lb. 60/70 Gulf shrimp, peeled
2 tbsp. crab boil or Old Bay Seasoning	1 lb. Louisiana crawfish tails
1 tbsp salt	1 lb. Louisiana crab claw meat or crab fingers
1 tbsp. black pepper	2 lb. fettuccine, boiled

Melt butter in a Dutch oven over medium heat. Sauté onion, celery, bell pepper, and garlic. When aromatics are translucent, add Worcestershire sauce and seasonings. Sauté for about 5 minutes. Add flour, stirring constantly to prevent sticking. When flour is fully incorporated and has absorbed the butter, add milk and cream. Stir over medium heat until mixture has thickened. Add grated Parmesan cheese and stir until melted and smooth. Fold in shrimp, crawfish, and crab. When shrimp is fully cooked, after about 20 minutes, the sauce is ready. Toss with fettuccine and serve.

Serves 12.

STUFFED PEPPERS

My recipe for stuffed peppers was derived by combining three different recipes representing separate times in my life. My mother and grandmother made stuffed peppers with ground beef. Mrs. Jesse Mae Allen, who worked at a local grocery store, added small shrimp. Mrs. Barbara Goia's Italian influence added Parmesan cheese. I like the marriage of these three distinct recipes. Some add rice, corn, and tomatoes, but I leave those out so as not to detract from the meat.

4 whole green bell peppers
2 cups diced onions
1 cup diced celery
2 cups diced bell peppers
2 tbsp. Circle Z Seasoning Mix
  (see Index)
3 lb. ground beef
1 lb. 60/70 shrimp, peeled
½ cup Parmesan cheese
½ cup Italian breadcrumbs
2 tbsp. Worcestershire sauce
1 egg

Breadcrumb Topping
½ stick butter, melted
½ cup grated Parmesan cheese
½ cup Italian breadcrumbs

Preheat oven to 425 degrees. Cut bell peppers in half lengthwise and remove seeds and membrane. Arrange on a baking sheet and roast in the oven for 20 minutes. Once peppers are nicely roasted, remove from oven and set aside to cool. Reduce oven temperature to 350 degrees.

While peppers are roasting, in a large pot, sauté onions, diced peppers, and celery with seasoning mix until onions are translucent. Add ground beef and shrimp. When beef is browned, mix in Parmesan cheese, breadcrumbs, Worcestershire sauce, and egg.

In a separate bowl make the breadcrumb topping. Mix melted butter, grated Parmesan cheese, and Italian breadcrumbs. Fill cooled pepper halves with stuffing and sprinkle with breadcrumb topping. Bake for 20 minutes at 350 degrees until tops are golden brown.

Makes 8 bell pepper halves.

TIP:

THE TASTE OF THE RIBS IMPROVES IF RUB IS APPLIED THE DAY BEFORE AND THE RIBS ARE ALLOWED TO MARINATE IN THE FLAVORS. WHILE YOU ARE GRILLING, THROW A COUPLE POUNDS OF ANY OF WAYNE JACOB'S SAUSAGES ON THE GRILL AND BASTE WITH SAUCE.

Every Mother's Day, my family holds a barbecue and gives the ladies the day off. In the city, restaurants are busy with families taking mothers out, but in the country, it's a great day for a cookout. Always on the menu were ribs, Wayne Jacob's smoked sausage and hot sausage, chicken, baked beans, potato salad, tomato cucumber salad, and garlic bread.

People are often intimidated by ribs because they do not have the patience to let them cook slowly. To help make this recipe simpler, I start with the same rub/seasoning for ribs, baked beans, and sauce and prepare the rub in advance. The night before your barbecue, soak your navy beans in water to cut down on the cooking time.

Rib Rub

2 cups brown sugar	½ cup Circle Z Seasoning Mix
2 tbsp. chili powder	(see Index)
1 tbsp. cumin	1 tbsp. celery salt
1 tbsp. smoked paprika	

Combine all ingredients and store in an airtight container.

Makes about 3 cups.

Beans

6 slices Wayne Jacob's bacon, chopped	¼ cup rib rub mixture
	3 oz. tomato paste
1 onion, chopped	1 lb. navy beans, soaked overnight then drained

In a 6 quart oven-safe pot, render chopped bacon over medium heat. Add onion and sauté until translucent. Add rib rub and tomato paste, stirring constantly for about 5 minutes to allow the paste to caramelize and the spices to bloom. Add the drained beans to the pot. Stir in 3 quarts of warm water. Bring to a boil, cover the pot, and place covered pot in a 350 degree oven. Bake for 2 hours while you prepare the ribs.

Serves 6.

Barbecue Sauce

1 onion, chopped
¼ cup butter
3 oz. tomato paste
½ cup apple cider vinegar
½ cup molasses
½ cup rib rub mix
1 tbsp. mustard seed

In a 3 quart pot, sauté onion in butter until caramelized. Add remaining ingredients and cook over medium heat until incorporated and bubbling. Add 3 cups water and simmer for about 30 minutes until thick.

Makes 1 quart.

Ribs

2 whole racks baby back pork ribs
1½ cups rib rub
1 cup apple cider vinegar
2 cups homemade barbecue sauce

Preheat grill to about 400 degrees. Wash ribs and pat dry. Remove the membrane from the bone side and cover thoroughly with rib rub. Transfer to a hot grill and caramelize ribs about 3-5 minutes per side. Baste with apple cider vinegar and then rotate ribs to caramelize the other side. Remove ribs from the grill, baste once more, and wrap with foil. Reduce the heat of the grill to about 250 degrees or move ribs so that they cook over indirect heat. Allow ribs to cook undisturbed for 60-90 minutes, depending on how tender you like them. Remove ribs from the foil and brush on barbecue sauce. Return to the grill for another 10 minutes to caramelize the sauce.

Serves 6.

BANANA CREAM CHEESE PIE

Mama Winnie, my grandmother on my mother's side, always served one of these pies at her family dinners. In fact, it seems she always kept one on hand in the refrigerator. She would top half with crushed pineapple for my grandfather and the other half with cherry pie filling for my father, her son-in-law. While some in-laws never like the spouses of their kids, my grandparents seemed to love them more than their own offspring.

Graham Cracker Crust

1½ cups ground graham crackers
½ cup sugar
¼ cup melted butter

Filling

16 oz. cream cheese
½ cup heavy cream
14 oz. sweetened condensed milk
½ cup lemon juice
1 tsp. pure vanilla
2 ripe bananas

Preheat oven to 350 degrees. To prepare the crust combine graham crackers, sugar, and butter. Press into a pie pan and bake for 15 minutes. For the filling, cream the cream cheese in a stand mixer, scraping the sides of the bowl with a spatula. Slowly add heavy cream and condensed milk, then beat in lemon juice and vanilla. Slice bananas into the baked pie crust and cover with filling. Refrigerate until completely set, about 2 hours.

Makes 1 pie.

LEMON ICE BOX PIE

This is an easy and delicious dessert. It follows the same recipe as key lime pie but substitutes lemon. My mom used to make individual ones to sell at swim meets. They were all gone by the time I was out of the pool.

Crust
2 cups graham cracker crumbs
1 cup sugar
½ cup butter, melted
1 tsp. cinnamon
1 tsp. salt

Filling
14 oz. canned condensed milk
½ cup lemon juice
1 lemon, zested
2 egg yolks

Topping
1 cup heavy whipping cream
1 cup powdered sugar
1 tsp. vanilla

Preheat oven to 350 degrees. Combine all crust ingredients in a mixing bowl then press into a 9 inch pie pan or tarte pan. Bake for 15 minutes. Remove from oven and allow to cool.

Once crust has cooled, whisk together all filling ingredients and pour into cooled pie crust. Bake for 30 minutes, until pie is just set around the edges and slightly jiggly in the middle. Remove from oven. The pie will set as it cools. Allow pie to cool completely before adding the topping.

Use a hand mixer to whisk together topping ingredients until stiff peaks form. Spread or pipe onto pie and refrigerate for at least 2 hours before serving.

Makes 1 pie.

TIP:
THIS PIE MAY ALSO BE FROZEN FOR AN ICE CREAM PIE-TYPE DESSERT.

COCONUT CAKE

I love this recipe because the cake is light and very moist. The icing has a hint of lemon that balances out the sweetness of the coconut.

Cake

5 eggs, separated
1 cup butter, room temperature
2 cups sugar
½ cup vegetable oil
2 cups unbleached flour
1 tsp. baking soda
1 cup buttermilk
3 cups shredded coconut

Frosting

16 oz. cream cheese, room temperature
1 cup butter, room temperature
1 lemon, zested and juiced
3¼ cups powdered sugar
3 cups toasted shredded coconut

Preheat oven to 325 degrees. Line three 9 inch cake pans with waxed paper and grease with cooking spray. In the bowl of a stand mixer with whisk attachment, beat egg whites on high for about 30 seconds to one minute, until stiff peaks form. Do not overbeat. Transfer to a separate bowl and set aside. With the stand mixer, cream butter and sugar until fluffy. Mix in oil. Add egg yolks one at a time and beat well after each addition. In a separate bowl, sift together flour and baking soda. Alternating, add buttermilk and dry ingredients to the wet mixture. Fold in coconut. Fold in beaten egg whites a third at a time. Divide batter evenly between 3 greased and lined baking pans. Bake for 25 minutes or until a toothpick comes out clean. When completely cooled, turn out onto cake platter to frost.

While the cake is cooling, in a stand mixer or with a hand mixer, cream the cream cheese and butter together until smooth. Mix in the lemon zest and juice. Add the powdered sugar and beat together until fully incorporated. Frost with an offset spatula, then cover the entire cake with toasted coconut.

Makes 1 3-layer cake.

MUSCADINE JAM

As a kid, I always looked forward to visiting my aunt and uncle's farm in Abita Springs, about an hour north of New Orleans. There were two ponds to fish, a goat, chickens, and a long fence of muscadine vines. I don't think they ever made anything with them, but I loved to eat the fruit.

I've had muscadine jam from various sources, but many times I'm disappointed that the jam doesn't capture the essence and nuanced flavor of the actual fruit. While some jam recipes call for added pectin, I've never had much luck with that ingredient. Instead, I usually cook apples with the muscadines to provide pectin without influencing the flavor.

2 gallons muscadines
2 cups lemon juice, divided
1 lemon, zested
2½ lb. apples, peeled, cored,
 and sliced
6 cups sugar

In a large bowl, squeeze 2 gallons of muscadines to separate skins from pulp. Add both skins and pulp to a large stainless steel pot over medium heat. Boil muscadines with 1 cup lemon juice and lemon zest for 1 hour. Strain the mixture through a mesh strainer or food mill to remove seeds and large pieces of pulp and skin. Retain the juice and discard the pulp. Clean pot thoroughly.

In the cleaned pot, combine strained juice, apples, sugar, and 1 cup lemon juice and cook for 2 hours over medium heat. When jam is done, the apples will have cooked and balls of jelly will be forming in the mixture. Puree if you prefer a smooth consistency. Ladle into sterilized jars while hot and follow safety rules for canning.

Makes 4 quarts.

PRESERVED FIGS

Mama Bell picked, cooked, and canned pears, peaches, and figs. The figs were my favorite. The syrup was so thick and sweet, and on vanilla ice cream it hardened to something like taffy. Almost 20 years went by before I attempted to cook my own figs. My grandmother was gone so I asked Ms. Irene Rauch for her recipe. She guided me through the whole process like a pro. They came out just like I'd remembered.

8 cups fresh figs
4 cups sugar
1 lemon, juiced
1 lemon rind

In an 8 quart pot, combine all ingredients with 1 gallon of water and bring to a boil. Boil for 2 hours. Syrup will be thick and amber in color. Figs will be translucent. Ladle into sterilized jars while hot and follow safety rules for canning.

Makes 8 pints.

FALL

During fall in South Louisiana, we look forward to pecans, smoked meats, citrus, mirliton, green beans, pumpkins, yams, and oysters.

Taking advantage of the mild weather, my dad's second crop of Creole tomatoes grows as fast as it can to beat the first frost. Sugarcane is starting to bend at its base under the weight of its own sugar. Green beans, yellow squash, and okra still thrive, while yams, mirliton, and pumpkins ripen in the late summer sun. Pecans fatten on the trees. Citrus is so abundant that the branches sometimes crack from the weight of the ripening fruit. And as the days get shorter, we start to plan our winter garden.

Most importantly for us at Wayne Jacob's Smokehouse: smoked meat season is here. My dad and I, just as generations have before us, have been cutting and splitting wood all summer to prepare. Personally, I cook gumbo and jambalaya year-round, but many people in the River Parishes wait for the first cold front to arrive before preparing these iconic dishes. At Wayne Jacob's Smokehouse, we have to keep a close eye on the weather forecast to decide how much meat to produce so that we can keep local cravings satisfied. In the off-season we produce 200 pounds of andouille per week. Between mid-October and Mardi Gras, we can sell 500 pounds of andouille per day—if we can keep up. Not only do we sell out of andouille, we have trouble keeping smoked sausage, tasso, smoked chicken, turkey necks, hog head cheese, cracklin', and boudin in stock. We have smokehouses filled around the clock between Halloween and New Year's.

When much of the country is gearing up for a cold winter, we are celebrating our break from the summer heat. Food festivals, football tailgating, and cooking contests are reason enough to get out the giant black iron pots, grills, and smoked meats so that we can cook outside with friends and a few beers. These celebrations provide a needed break from the anticipation of the fall harvest but are tempered by the impending work of picking, processing, and preserving all of it.

SWEET AND SPICY PECANS

My mother's parents, Philip and Winnie Chauvin, lived on the Chauvin family farm in Edgard, Louisiana. This is where my mom grew up surrounded by her first cousins and extended family. I was also fortunate to grow up with my cousins as my closest friends. It was always great when Mama Winnie would let me spend the night at their house. We'd stay up late to watch *20/20* or *Murder, She Wrote*. They had no air conditioning when I was young, so we slept with the windows open. I'd hear cars passing on the River Road and the horns of tugboats in the Mississippi on foggy nights. I'd wake up late, and Mama Winnie would usually have sweet cornbread with butter and a cup of coffee milk for me and Papa Philip. I'd eat my breakfast and then I'd head out to explore and to see what my cousins were up to. If they weren't home, I'd head out to pick pecans.

My great-grandparents had four giant pecan trees on their property. Usually they had been picked over, but my eight-year-old self was determined to find every last one. I'd give them to my great-grandmother to use. She'd have knee-high stockings filled with pecans hanging on the back porch to dry, and the kitchen table always looked like someone had just taken a break from cracking and cleaning pecans.

When I opened Vacherie Restaurant, I remembered how much those times with my great-grandparents meant to me so I put an appetizer of Sweet and Spicy Pecans on the menu to remind me of those Saturday mornings on the Chauvin farm.

2 lb. pecan halves	1 tsp. cayenne pepper
2 egg whites	5 dashes Tabasco
¼ cup molasses	1 tbsp. kosher salt
½ cup dark brown sugar	1 tbsp. chili powder
¼ cup melted butter	1 tbsp. paprika

Spread pecan halves on a lined sheet pan. Bake for 20 minutes in a 250 degree oven. Meanwhile, whisk egg whites in a large bowl until foamy. Whisk in remaining ingredients. Remove baked pecans from the oven and add to the egg white mixture. Stir to coat evenly and spread on baking sheet. Return pecans to the oven for 1 hour, stirring after 30 minutes. Remove from the oven and cool completely before storing.

Makes 2 quarts.

TIP:
THE ROASTED BEETS CAN
BE PREPARED A DAY IN
ADVANCE AND STORED IN THE
REFRIGERATOR.

ROASTED BEET, SATSUMA, GOAT CHEESE, AND TOASTED PECAN SALAD

Be aware that anytime an old farmer asks, "You wanna take a few beets, turnips, or carrots with you when you go?" what they really mean is "Let's go into the garden and fill the back of your truck with vegetables, greens, dirt, and all."

This salad is a flavorful fall or even winter recipe, depending on how cold the weather gets. Beet season overlaps with Louisiana citrus and the two make a great pairing. Beets are delicious and very easy to grow, but they can be messy because they turn everything they touch red. Rather than peeling them and boiling much of the flavor out of them, I like to roast them to concentrate the taste of the beet.

6 beets
4 cups arugula (optional)
4 satsumas or mandarins, peeled
  and segmented
3 oz. goat cheese
¼ cup chopped pecans

Citrus Vinaigrette
3 tbsp. red wine vinegar
1 tbsp. Creole mustard
3 tbsp. satsuma juice
1 tsp. salt
1 tsp. black pepper
1 egg yolk
½ cup canola or light olive oil
½ red onion, thinly sliced

In a 350 degree oven, roast beets on a baking sheet for about an hour. When done they should give a little when squeezed and a knife should be able to pierce them easily. Allow them to cool completely before peeling.

While the beets are cooling, prepare the citrus vinaigrette. Combine all vinaigrette ingredients except the oil and onion then slowly whisk in the oil to emulsify. Stir the sliced onion into the dressing and let sit for 30 minutes. This will mellow the taste of the onion.

Plate the arugula (if using) and then neatly arrange the citrus segments, goat cheese, and pecans. Top with the roasted beats and drizzle with vinaigrette.

Serves 6.

OYSTER TASSO ARTICHOKE SOUP

In South Louisiana, we especially enjoy our oysters raw, but we also love them fried on po' boys, charbroiled, in dressings, and in gumbos and soups. The tradition is to eat oysters only in months with an "R" in them. Before refrigerated trucks and pasteurization, eating oysters in warmer months was unsafe. In the spring and summer, the water warms, and algae and bacteria bloom in warm conditions. Oysters, because they are nature's filters and consist mostly of water, are especially susceptible to bacteria growth. When the water is cooler, in the months that have an "R" in them, the oysters are safe to eat. This is a great example of eating seasonally.

Tasso is another southern Louisiana favorite. When using tasso, there are two things to remember:

1. A little goes a long way. Tasso is very spicy and very smoky.

2. You will get the most flavor out of your tasso if you fry it in your roux and aromatics before adding any liquid. This process will render its smoky fat and bloom the spices.

1 onion, diced	2 tbsp. cup flour
1 red pepper, seeded and diced	12 oz. canned artichoke hearts,
1 cup chopped green onions	quartered and undrained
1 tbsp. chopped garlic	1 pint of oysters with liquid
¼ cup diced tasso	3 cups milk
½ stick butter	½ cup heavy cream
1 tbsp. Worcestershire sauce	1 cup chopped fresh parsley
2 tbsp. Circle Z Seasoning Mix	¼ cup grated Parmesan cheese
(see Index)	French bread for serving

Sauté onion, red pepper, green onions, garlic, and tasso in butter. Add Worcestershire sauce and seasonings; simmer about 5 minutes to allow the spices to bloom. Add flour and stir to incorporate. Mix in artichoke hearts, oysters, milk, and heavy cream. Simmer for 10 minutes then whisk in parsley and grated Parmesan cheese. Serve with buttered and toasted French bread.

Serves 6-8.

MAMA BELL'S WHITE BEAN AND POTATO SOUP

My grandmother, Anabell Schexnayder Zeringue, or Mama Bell as we called her, cooked a pot of white beans every week of her adult life until Alzheimer's disease took that ability from her. So through the course of 65 years, at least one pot per week, about two pounds per pot, 52 weeks per year equals around 6,760 pounds of white beans cooked in a lifetime. Needless to say, they were the best. They were famous in Vacherie and Wallace, mostly because I bragged to my friends' grandmas about them. Mama Bell was not happy that I was telling her business on the street. She was a very private person.

Sometimes even she got tired of eating the same beans and rice so she would mix it up and make a soup. We always knew we had an amazing treat in store when Mama Bell would call and say that she had cooked something for us. Sometimes it was *riz au lait* (imagine the marriage of rice pudding and eggnog); sometimes it was her T-Gateau (iced tea cookies); but I especially loved when it was her delicious white bean and potato soup. Usually in the winter or during Lent, she would prepare a huge Tupperware container for each of her children's families. She also sent us home with a Bunny Bread bag filled with bread that had been toasted until it was the texture of croutons. As much as we all enjoyed her cooking, I really didn't appreciate how much effort all of that took until I started catering myself.

1 lb. dried white beans
4 cups diced onions
1 cup chopped green onions
1 lb. red potatoes, diced
1 chicken bouillon cube
1 tbsp. cup tomato paste
2 tbsp. Circle Z Seasoning Mix (see Index)
1 cup chopped parsley

In a large pot soak white beans in water overnight. Drain water and replace with 2 gallons of clean water. Add diced onions and green onions to beans and cover. Cook over medium heat until beans are creamy and tender, about 2 hours. Puree beans with an immersion blender. Add diced potatoes, chicken bouillon, tomato paste, seasoning mix, and parsley. Simmer until potatoes are tender, about 20 minutes, stirring often. Serve with croutons.

Serves 8.

Navy Beans

La. 2### NET WT. 2#

KEEP UNDER REFRIGERATION

349

PACKED BY

B & C SEAFOOD, INC.

VACHERIE, LA 70090   (225) 265-3###

SWEET POTATO AND ANDOUILLE SOUP

Andouille is the cornerstone of Wayne Jacob's Smokehouse. It is all-natural pork, hand butchered, and coarsely ground. We use only natural beef casing. Each link weighs 1-1½ pounds. We do not use any preservatives, additives, or artificial flavors in our andouille, which is smoked for hours with real wood smoke and is fully cooked.

Traditional dishes in which we feature andouille are gumbos, stews, and jambalayas. We also cut it thin to fry as chips. We use it in pasta sauces, in soups, and on salads. It finds its way onto charcuterie boards, and we incorporate it into dishes in any way that can be imagined.

This Sweet Potato and Andouille Soup is a great soup for a cold day. A nice mix of the sweet, spicy, and smoky, it contains all the flavors I associate with fall and winter in South Louisiana. It will warm your body and your soul. This recipe makes a lot so invite family and friends to share.

½ stick butter
3 cups chopped leeks
2 cups diced onions
1 cup chopped green onions
1 red pepper, seeded and sliced
½ andouille link, sliced
½ cup dark brown sugar
2 large sweet potatoes, peeled and cubed
1 quart chicken stock
1½ tbsp. Circle Z Seasoning Mix (see Index)
½ cup heavy cream

Melt butter in an 8-quart pot over medium heat. Add leeks, onions, green onions, red pepper, and andouille. Sauté until vegetables are soft. Mix in brown sugar and sweet potatoes. Carefully add chicken stock and stir to incorporate. Bring to a boil then reduce heat to medium and cook until potatoes are fork tender. Puree with an immersion blender. Stir in heavy cream and simmer for 10 minutes. Serve immediately.

Serves 6-8.

WAYNE JACOB'S SMOKEHOUSE

Wayne Jacob's Smokehouse and Restaurant is located in the old Milesville area of Laplace, Louisiana, a short drive west of New Orleans. Nolan "Nat" Jacob opened the business on April 1, 1950, as a general store with a focus on andouille. As a teenager he—like many other budding andouille makers—learned his craft at the Alexander Brothers General Store across the street from the lot where he would one day build his own shop. Many of his peers also graduated from Alexander Brothers to open their own markets and produce their own versions of the local specialty. With so many shops selling smoked meats, Laplace became known as the "Andouille Capital of the World." Some of the stores were seasonal, and some closed after national grocery chains moved in, but Wayne Jacob's Smokehouse remains.

Nat Jacob raised his family in the apartment above the shop so that he could always be close enough to man the smokehouse. His children also worked in the shop, which operated as a full grocery store, until his son Wayne took over the business and decided to run it seasonally from October through Christmas. Passed down through the generations with great attention to the tradition and quality standards of its founder, today Wayne Jacob's Smokehouse continues the history of smoking and producing the highest quality artisan-smoked meats and fresh sausage.

Andouille is the cornerstone of our business. During the fall, by far our busiest season, we produce, by hand, more than 500 pounds of andouille per day and sell out daily. Our sausage is all-natural pork, hand butchered and coarsely ground, with each link weighing between a pound and a pound and a half. We use only natural beef casing. We do not use any preservatives, additives, or artificial flavors in our andouille.

The only ingredients are pork, salt, pepper, garlic, natural casing, time, and care. As with all smoking, the key to great andouille is low and slow. Our andouille is smoked for hours over a low heat with real wood smoke.

Andouille, smoked sausage, tasso, and other original recipes continue to draw the community to Wayne Jacob's. I'm proud to be the owner of the only place where three generations of my family have purchased smoked meats.

We are extremely fortunate that every successive owner of the smokehouse has had such an appreciation of and respect for the quality of the handmade products we make. The business has grown with each subsequent owner into a year-round smokehouse, restaurant, and online market. We have shipped to all states and many countries, but our main goal has always been to serve the community that has supported us for more than 70 years.

TURTLE SAUCE PIQUANTE

The St. Philip Food Festival was an especially exciting time of year for me as a child. Not only could I put off doing my homework for the week leading up to the festival because I had to help my dad set up, but it was also usually held on my birthday weekend. Thinking back on the menu, I realize that it would be very hard to replicate today. The offerings were full of fresh and local seafood, produce, and wild game, all of it harvested, hunted, and cooked by members of the church. They donated all the food, plus their time, energy, and most importantly their expertise in preparing the meals for the greater good of the church parish: turtle sauce piquante, deer sauce piquante, seafood gumbo, chicken and andouille gumbo, crawfish fettuccine, crawfish étouffée, shrimp Creole, jambalaya, po' boys, fried des Allemands catfish, pralines, divinity fudge, and beautifully decorated and delicious homemade cakes that could be purchased whole or by the slice.

The auction was equally interesting. Nowadays we auction off gift cards, art, or vacations. We rarely see auctions for locally produced softshell crabs, softshell crawfish, river shrimp, alligator meat, whole pigs, handmade furniture, vegetables, cooked food, desserts, candies, or a giant live snapping turtle. So many of those skills and talents have been taken to the grave, but that sense of community in the name of service continues to inspire me.

I've read that just as we know chicken and turkey to have white meat and dark meat, turtle has seven different grades of meat. That being said, there is a lot of connective tissue that can be impossible to eat if cooked incorrectly. Many recipes call for boiling the meat until tender and to make a stock. I prefer a browning and braising method. Besides boiling pasta and maybe blanching vegetables, in my opinion, boiling usually removes flavors by watering down and washing away. Browning, roasting, frying, and braising concentrate flavors by removing water or release flavor by rendering fats. It takes the same amount of time as boiling and the end result is a richer flavor with tender meat.

This recipe is large because when I buy local turtle meat, it is packed in five-pound packs. So make a large pot and freeze leftovers, give some away, or cut the recipe in half. This recipe also works for wild game like alligator, deer, or squirrel. The braising will make such lean meats tender without drying them out.

5 lb. Louisiana snapping turtle meat
1½ cups canola oil
2 cups flour, divided
3 large onions, diced
3 bell peppers, seeded and diced
3 jalapeño peppers, seeded and diced
3 poblano peppers, seeded and diced (optional)
1 head of celery, diced
3 bunches green onions, chopped
3 bunches Italian parsley, chopped
12 cloves whole garlic, peeled
½ cup Circle Z Seasoning Mix (see Index)
¼ cup Worcestershire sauce
2 cups tomato paste
5 cups diced tomatoes
2 cups dry white wine
3 quarts chicken broth

Heat oven to 350 degrees. Cut turtle meat into uniform cubes (like stew meat), removing any major connective tissue. Don't worry about being too meticulous with this step because braising will melt away any remaining fat or tissue. Toss the meat with ½ cup flour.

In a large Dutch oven or iron pot, heat oil over medium heat. Brown meat in batches, being careful not to crowd the pot. Remove the browned turtle from the pot and set aside. Add the remaining flour to the pot to make a caramel-colored roux, stirring constantly for at least 20 minutes. Scrape the brown bits, or fond, from the bottom. When roux is caramel in color, add vegetables, seasonings, and Worcestershire sauce. Sauté until onions are translucent. Add tomato paste and cook for 5-10 minutes until paste begins to caramelize. Deglaze the pot with diced tomatoes and white wine. Scrape the bottom of the pot, releasing any remaining fond. Return the turtle meat, with its drippings, to the pot. Add the chicken broth. Stir to incorporate and bring to a boil. Cover and place the pot in the oven for 2 hours or until thickened and turtle meat falls apart.

Serves 20 people or makes 10 quarts.

MAMA WINNIE'S THANKSGIVING DINNER

Mama Winnie's cooking was the embodiment of heartwarming comfort food. You could tell that her cooking was thoughtful and gentle, and she took the time to tweak each of her recipes.

Thanksgiving was the perfect example of her style: simple ingredients cooked in the way that brought out the best flavor, as opposed to drowning out simple flavors with more ingredients.

POT ROASTED STICKY CHICKEN

Neither my mother nor my grandmother likes turkey. Even for Thanksgiving, turkey is out of the question in either of their kitchens. Instead, we always had pot roasted chicken, and for Thanksgiving it was stuffed with oyster dressing. It was so good that I don't think anyone ever mentioned the "T" word at the table.

1 whole chicken
2 tbsp. Circle Z Seasoning Mix (see Index)
½ cup flour
½ cup canola oil
1 onion, thinly sliced

Heat oven to 350 degrees. Wash chicken and pat dry. Cut into pieces and split each breast into 2 (to divide chicken into 10 pieces total) for even browning and cooking. Combine seasonings and flour in a shallow bowl and lightly dredge each piece of chicken in the seasoned flour. Reserve remaining seasoned flour for gravy.

Add oil to a heavy pan or Dutch oven over medium heat. Brown chicken pieces on all sides but be careful not to burn the fond, the chicken scraps, on the bottom of the pot. This will become the foundation of the gravy. Remove chicken from the pan and set aside. Add sliced onion to the pan with ½ cup water to deglaze and scrape the fond from the bottom. Whisk 1½ cups water with the remaining seasoned flour and add it to the pan with the onion. Return the chicken with its drippings to the pan. Bring to a boil. Cover and place into the preheated oven. Cook for 1 hour. Remove the cover and cook uncovered for 15 minutes to reduce the gravy. As the gravy reduces, it will become "sticky." The chicken will fall apart and will be tender and juicy.

Serves 4.

MEATY OYSTER DRESSING

Beef, pork, and oysters make up this hearty and rich dressing. It is great alone, over rice, or stuffed into a chicken.

This recipe is very similar to a recipe known as *la Vacherie farre*. Instead of using oysters, the recipe for farre would use chicken livers or gizzards. It is usually served over rice or spread on white bread for wedding sandwiches.

1 large onion, diced
6 stalks celery, chopped
2 bell peppers, chopped
2 cloves garlic, chopped
1 lb. ground beef
1 lb. ground pork
1 pint Louisiana oysters, chopped
Liquor reserved from oysters
4 tbsp. Circle Z Seasoning Mix (see Index)
½ cup Worcestershire sauce
2 cups Italian breadcrumbs

Breadcrumb Topping
3 tbsp. butter
1 cup Italian breadcrumbs

In a large pan over medium heat, combine onion, celery, peppers, and garlic and cook uncovered until translucent and starting to caramelize. Mix in ground beef and ground pork. When the meat is evenly browned, drain the fat. Stir in chopped oysters and half the oyster liquor. Add seasoning mix and cook until liquid has nearly evaporated, stirring often. Add Worcestershire sauce, remaining oyster liquor, and breadcrumbs and cook until thickened. In a separate bowl, make the breadcrumb topping by mixing breadcrumbs and melted butter until thoroughly combined. Transfer meat mixture to an oven-safe casserole dish, top with buttered breadcrumbs, and bake for 30 minutes at 350 degrees.

Makes 4 quarts.

ROUX PEAS

I don't often recommend using canned vegetables, but this recipe is an exception. I generally say that fresh is best with canned as a last resort. However, green English peas aren't grown here, and canned peas are inexpensive and will pass as a vegetable. My mother and grandmother always preferred Le Sueur Petit Pois for this recipe.

½ cup butter
½ cup flour
½ medium onion, diced
2 tsp. salt
2 tsp. black pepper
28 oz. canned petit pois; do not drain
1 tbsp. sugar

In a heavy-bottomed pot over medium heat, melt butter. Add flour and stir constantly for about 10 minutes to make a caramel-colored roux. Add onion to the roux and season with salt and pepper. Sauté until onions start to brown. Stir in peas with liquid and sugar. Simmer until thickened, about 20 minutes. Serve alone or over rice.

Serves 6.

TIP:

THIS RECIPE WORKS VERY WELL WITH EGGPLANT SUBSTITUTED FOR MIRLITON. FOR EGGPLANT, SKIP THE BOILING STAGE AND INTRODUCE THE CUBED RAW EGGPLANT TO THE SAUTÉING ONIONS.

MIRLITON WITH CRAB AND SHRIMP

Creole mirliton is a beautiful, fluted, light green fruit, a cousin to the chayote. When you can get it in the early fall, do not hesitate because the season ends as soon as the first frost hits. I have seen and tried recipes for mirliton in soups, fried mirliton, pickled mirliton, and even mirliton in pies. My great-grandmother, Esperance Leroux Chauvin, made stuffed mirliton with river shrimp. My Mama Winnie prepared it as a dressing, always present at her holiday table. The natural sweetness of the smothered mirliton and the river shrimp with the savory flavors of butter, onions, and breadcrumbs was the perfect balance of delicate flavors. It was a true testament to the mastery of generations using local, fresh, and seasonal ingredients. Getting the most flavor out of each ingredient by the way it is treated in preparation, rather than piling on ingredients, is one of the cornerstones of Cajun cooking.

The best way to ensure that you have access to all the mirlitons you need is to plant your own crop. Place your mirliton in a dark, dry place for the winter and allow it to sprout. After the last freeze (usually the first week of March and the same time you plant your tomatoes), plant sprouted mirlitons in a sunny but protected place with well-drained soil. Mound soil halfway up the fruit, leaving the top half exposed as well as the end of the sprout. Mulch the mound to prevent erosion. It is recommended that you bury a piece of rusty iron, such as a railroad spike, near the mirliton to aid in the health of the plant. Do not let any chickens around the new plants. I learned that the hard way. The vine will grow all summer and will produce small flowers before fruiting. A common misconception is that there are male and female plants. Mirliton is self-pollenating so you don't need more than one, but then again it doesn't hurt to have a backup.

5 lb. mirlitons
1 tbsp. salt
1 large onion, diced
1 bunch green onions, chopped
1 clove garlic, chopped
¼ cup butter
½ cup Italian breadcrumbs

½ cup grated Parmesan cheese
1 egg, beaten
3 tbsp. Circle Z Seasoning Mix
  (see Index)
1 lb. 60/70 shrimp, peeled
  and deveined
1 lb. Louisiana blue crab claw meat

Breadcrumb Topping

½ stick butter, melted
½ cup grated Parmesan cheese
½ cup Italian breadcrumbs

Cut each mirliton in half lengthwise and remove the seed. Place halves into a large pot, cover with water, and bring to a boil. Add salt and boil until mirlitons are fork tender. Drain and let cool. After mirlitons have cooled, chop roughly and set aside.

In a Dutch oven over medium heat, sauté onion, green onions, and garlic in butter until translucent. Add diced mirliton and cover, stirring occasionally. After the mirliton is smothered, about 30 minutes, remove from heat and mix in Italian breadcrumbs, grated Parmesan, and beaten egg. Season to taste with seasoning mix. Fold in raw shrimp and crab and transfer to a casserole dish.

In a separate bowl, make the breadcrumb topping. Combine melted butter, grated Parmesan cheese, and Italian breadcrumbs. Top mirlitons with breadcrumb topping and bake at 350 degrees until bubbly and golden.

Serves 12.

BAKED MACARONI AND CHEESE

Baked Macaroni and Cheese was always a staple on Mama Winnie's table. Even though I get negative reviews here and there from self-proclaimed macaroni purists, I always use spaghetti in my recipe. I do this to honor the home cooks and country restaurants that say, "Noodles are noodles." Although I didn't grow up in an Italian household, I do have an appreciation for the difference of noodle shapes for certain dishes—in fact, my house is built on the former site of the first macaroni factory in Louisiana—but the seafood markets and local grocery stores that sold plate lunches in my hometown used spaghetti, and so will I.

1 stick butter
¼ onion, diced
1 tbsp. salt
2 tsp. black pepper
2 tbsp. flour
4 cups milk
8 oz. cream cheese
4 cups grated sharp Cheddar cheese
½ cup grated Parmesan cheese
2 egg yolks
1 lb. spaghetti, boiled

Breadcrumb Topping
½ stick butter, melted
½ cup grated Parmesan cheese
½ cup Italian breadcrumbs

Preheat oven to 350 degrees. In an 8 quart pot, melt butter over medium heat. Sauté onion with salt and pepper until onion is translucent. Add flour and stir to incorporate. Whisk in milk and cream cheese. Whisk often to prevent sticking. When the mixture starts to thicken, after 5-10 minutes, whisk in Cheddar and Parmesan cheeses. Remove from the heat and whisk in egg yolks. Add boiled spaghetti to the pot and stir. In a separate bowl make the breadcrumb topping by mixing melted butter, grated Parmesan cheese, and Italian breadcrumbs. Transfer pasta to a 9x13 inch casserole dish, top with breadcrumb topping, and bake for 30 minutes or until bubbly.

Serves 12.

CANDIED LOUISIANA YAMS

I love a good sweet potato soufflé on my Thanksgiving plate as much as anyone. But as we all know, that Thanksgiving plate may lack a bit of texture with all of the casseroles that pop up on holiday menus. Many times, I find myself making my way through the potluck line not knowing which of the brown items I've already sampled and which I don't care to. This recipe keeps all of the ingredients identifiable, intact, and delicious.

6 Louisiana yams, peeled and cubed
1 cup sugar
1 tsp. vanilla
1 tsp. cinnamon
1 tsp. salt
24 oz. canned crushed pineapple with juice
¼ cup butter
1 cup chopped pecans
3 cups miniature marshmallows

Preheat oven to 350 degrees. In a large pot, boil yams for about 15 minutes until fork tender. Drain and transfer to a baking dish. In a medium-sized pot, bring sugar and 1 cup water to a boil to make simple syrup. Whisk vanilla, cinnamon, salt, and crushed pineapple together with syrup and pour over yams. Cut butter into pieces and sprinkle over yams. Top with pecans and marshmallows and bake until marshmallows are toasted, about 20 minutes

Serves 12.

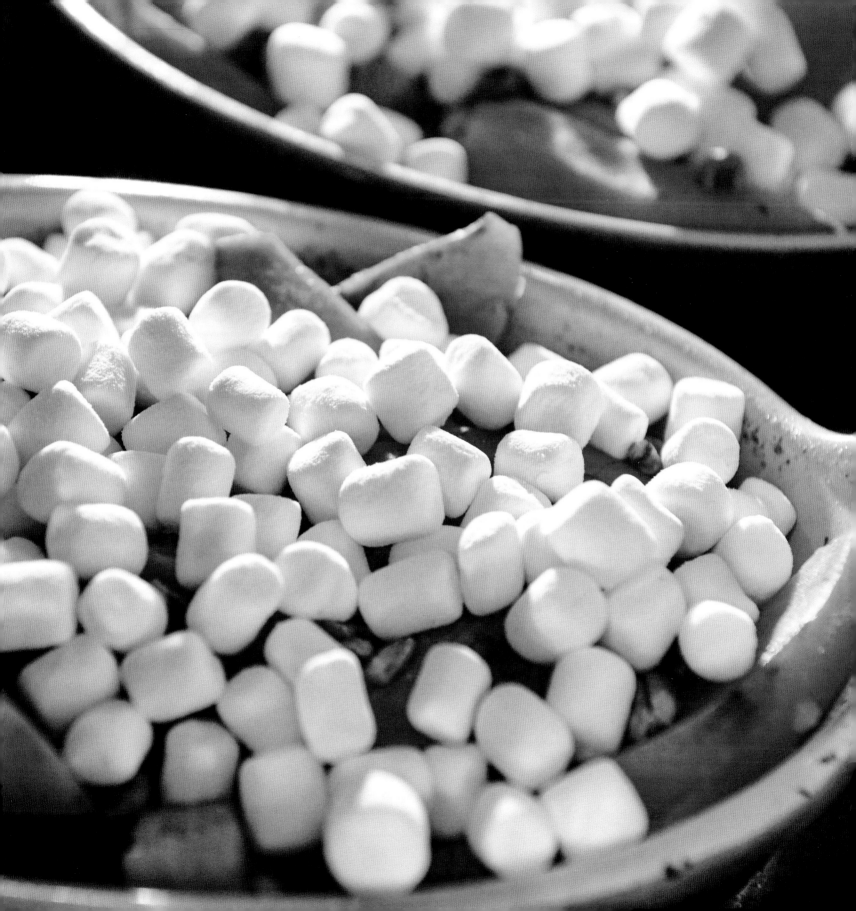

WJ'S BREAKFAST CASSEROLE

Casseroles don't always have to be a pile of mush. This one is more like a cheesy sausage quiche in a hash brown crust. Hear that, all you people with gluten issues! Baking the hash brown crust first is key to keeping a crispy crust. Sautéing your vegetables with the sausage will bring out the smokiness as well as eliminate the extra water that can ruin the custard. I've also learned over many tries that adding extra egg yolks to the custard will provide a much smoother and lighter texture. You can adapt the fillings to your liking.

Crust

2 russet potatoes
⅓ onion, diced (reserve remaining
⅔ onion for casserole filling)

3 tbsp. butter, melted
1 tsp. salt
1 tsp. black pepper

Filling

⅔ onion, diced
1 bunch green onions, chopped
1 bell pepper (red or green)
1 link Wayne Jacob's smoked
    sausage, sliced into rounds
1 tbsp. Circle Z Seasoning Mix
    (see Index)

1 tbsp. Worcestershire sauce
1 tbsp. butter
2 cups shredded Cheddar or pepper
    Jack cheese
8 eggs
4 egg yolks
3 cups half-and-half

Preheat oven to 425 degrees. Grate unpeeled potatoes into a colander or bowl. Wash the grated potatoes well with cold water and then wring them out as much as possible. This step gets rid of most of the excess starch, which would keep the potatoes from forming a crispy crust, and wringing out the water allows the potatoes and onions to fry instead of bake or steam.

Place potatoes into a mixing bowl, add diced onion, and mix in the melted butter, salt, and pepper. Pour the potato mixture into a 9x13 inch baking dish. Pat the potatoes down and along the sides of the pan to form a crust. Bake for 30 minutes, until golden.

In a skillet over high heat, sauté onion, green onions, bell pepper, smoked sausage, seasoning mix, and Worcestershire sauce in butter until onion is translucent and sausage is fragrant and starting to render. Remove from heat and pour into the baked hash brown crust. Top with shredded cheese.

In a separate bowl, whisk together eggs, egg yolks, and half-and-half. Pour mixture into the baking dish. Bake for 30 minutes or until set.

Serves 12.

PERFECT GRITS

I often hear arguments about whether a dish should be considered "Southern" or "Cajun." More often than not, the argument can be settled with one question: Are you from north or south of I-10? It seems that Interstate 10 works as a dividing line between many things. To the south, people tend to like salt in their grits, while north of I-10 the preference for sugar is more prevalent. This theory applies to other recipes as well: sweet cornbread to the south, salty to the north; chicken and dumplings north of the interstate, chicken fricassee south of the interstate; white gravy up north, rice and gravy down south.

That being said, salt is the most important ingredient in good grits south of I-10. My secret is that salt and butter are to be added to the cooking water of grits before the grits are whisked in. This lets the salty water actually hydrate the grits. As with salting pasta water, grits water should have the same salinity as tears. The cooks in my restaurants never forget that rule of thumb. You should also have enough water to actually hydrate the grits so that they are creamy, not sandy and undercooked. I finish my grits off with a bit of heavy cream.

½ cup butter
1 tsp. salt
1 cup grits
¼ cup heavy cream

Bring 5 cups water, butter, and salt to a boil. Whisk in grits and reduce heat to a simmer. Cook for about 10 minutes, stirring often to prevent sticking. When grits are thick and creamy, whisk in heavy cream and serve.

Serves 4.

Grit Cakes

1 batch grits	Green onions to taste
2 eggs	Sauteed mushrooms to taste
Shredded cheese to taste	Corn to taste

To make grit cakes, whisk eggs into warm grits. Mix in shredded cheese, green onions, sautéed mushrooms, corn, or any other fillings you desire. Pour onto a baking sheet (with sides) and place in the refrigerator to set. To ensure that the cakes heat evenly, make sure they are no thicker than 1 inch. After the grits have fully cooled, cut into any shape you choose. Dip cakes in egg wash then flour or biscuit mix. Pan fry in a little butter or oil until golden. Use as a base for grillades, seafood, pulled pork, or stews.

WINNIE'S DEVIL'S FOOD CAKE

Mama Winnie's Devil's Food Cake isn't exactly what we think of when we imagine modern-day devil's food. It contains cocoa but only as much as a red velvet cake. The flavor of the cake is mild, but the frosting is a buttery fudge that will harden like candy. In fact, I use the frosting recipe as a base for when I make fudge or pralines. Cooking the frosting to the right temperature and working quickly are the keys to making a beautiful and delicious cake.

3 cups flour
3 tsp. baking powder
1 cup butter
2 cups sugar
4 eggs
1 cup milk
2 tsp. vanilla
1 tsp. cocoa

Blonde Fudge Icing
2 cups sugar
1 cup PET milk
½ cup butter

In a mixing bowl, sift flour and baking powder together and set aside. In a separate large mixing bowl, cream butter and sugar until light and fluffy. Add eggs one at a time, beating well after each addition. Alternately add flour and milk, beating just until smooth after each ingredient is added. Stir in vanilla and cocoa. Pour batter into two greased 9-inch cake pans and bake at 350 degrees for 30 minutes or until a toothpick inserted in the middle of the cake comes out clean. Remove from the oven and allow to cool for 10 minutes before turning the cake layers out onto a cooling rack. Let layers cool completely before icing.

To make the icing, combine sugar, PET milk, and butter in a pot and, stirring frequently, cook over medium heat until mixture begins to separate from the bottom of the pot when stirred (similar to a hard ball stage). Remove from heat and beat by hand until mixture begins to thicken. Spread on cake immediately.

Serves 12.

PECAN PIE

As sugarcane farmers, we received a gallon each of molasses and cane syrup from the mill each year as a thank-you. I liked to use a little of that molasses in my pecan pie to complement the toasted pecans because they are both flavors of the fall.

9 inch pie shell
2 cups chopped pecans
1 cup dark corn syrup
¼ cup molasses
3 eggs
¾ cup sugar
¼ cup butter, melted
½ tsp. salt

Preheat oven to 325 degrees. Dock (or prick) pie shell with a fork, pour in chopped pecans, and bake for 10 minutes. The pecans will not only serve as pie weights, but they will also toast while the shell bakes. While shell is baking, mix together remaining ingredients. Remove pie shell from oven and let cool for 10 minutes. Top toasted pecans with filling mixture. Bake for 45 minutes or until completely set and slightly puffed. Remove from oven and let cool at least 2 hours before serving.

Serves 8.

PINEAPPLE UPSIDE-DOWN CAKE

Pineapple Upside-Down Cake is one of my favorite desserts. It transports me back to my childhood, sitting at Mama Bell's table with a big square of cake and a cold glass of milk. This is her recipe.

28 oz. canned pineapple rings with juice
1 small jar cherries
¼ cup butter
1 cup packed brown sugar

Cake

3 cups cake flour
2 tsp. baking powder
¾ tsp. baking soda
1 tsp. kosher salt
1 cup + 2 tbsp. butter
2 cups sugar
4 eggs
2 tsp. vanilla extract
1½ cups buttermilk

Preheat oven to 350 degrees. Line a 9x13 inch baking dish with parchment. Oil the parchment liberally and line with pineapple rings and cherries. In a small saucepan over low heat, combine butter, brown sugar, and pineapple juice. Simmer until the juice has been reduced by half to make a syrup. Pour syrup over pineapple in the baking dish.

To make the cake, sift flour, baking powder, baking soda, and salt together in a mixing bowl and set aside. In the bowl of a stand mixer, cream butter and sugar on high for about 5 minutes until light and fluffy. Reduce speed to medium and add ¼ cup of the flour mixture. Add eggs one at a time, beating well after each addition. Add vanilla and beat for 5 more minutes. Reduce speed to low and alternately add flour mixture and buttermilk, beating just until smooth. Pour batter over pineapple in the baking dish and spread to cover evenly. Bake for 1 hour or until a toothpick comes out clean when inserted in the center. When completely cooled turn out onto pan, carefully remove the parchment paper, and serve.

Serves 12.

INDEX

About Jarred and His Smokehouse

Chef Jarred Zeringue's family has lived, worked, and farmed in the River Parishes of Louisiana and nearby New Orleans since the early 1700s. Today the dishes that Chef Zeringue serves reflect the blend of cultures and influences shaped by the rich ancestry of the residents of South Louisiana.

A native of Vacherie, Louisiana, Jarred splits his time between the New Orleans French Quarter and Wayne Jacob's Smokehouse & Restaurant in LaPlace, a longstanding stop on the famed Andouille Trail.

Serving the residents of South Louisiana since 1950, Wayne Jacob's smokes meats the old-fashioned way with the same attention to detail and quality that its founder prized decades ago. Today, Jarred continues that tradition with pride, producing artisan smoked meats and fresh sausage while sharing the taste, flavors, and charm of Louisiana's culinary heritage.